ANDERS **INDSET**

WILD KNOWLEDGE

OUTTHINK THE REVOLUTION

ADVANCED PRAISE

"Let yourselves be seduced by this passionate manifesto about our fast-paced world. Who better than Anders Indset to write this inspiring eye-opener on bridging the gap between philosophy, business and ... Rock'n'Roll? You will be fascinated by this journey through science, technology, philosophy and the beauty of thinking."

Professor Yves Pigneur, University of Lausanne, Author with Alex Osterwalder of *Business Model Generation* and listed on Thinkers50

"*Wild Knowledge* offers important perspective on the role of business in the knowledge society."

Richard Florida, author *Rise of the Creative Class* and listed on Thinkers50 2015

"A passionate manifesto about our fast-paced world. Anders opens possibilities for solving today's challenges by changing how we think. *Wild Knowledge* shows that how we think shapes how we act, and only by shifting how we think can we truly innovate and be ready for what's coming at us in the 21st Century."

Amy C. Edmondson, Novartis Professor of Leadership and Management, author, *Building the future*

"*Wild Knowledge* offers important perspective on the role of business in the knowledge society."

Richard Florida, author *Rise of the Creative Class*

"The wheel of information now spins so fast that most of us live in a blur. How can we thrive in this disoriented state? Anders Indset's optimistic rallying cry is that yes, we can out-think the rapid change and disruption around us – and we must, if we are going to manage the future intelligently."
Marshall Goldsmith, executive coach, business educator and *New York Times* bestselling author, ranked the number one leadership thinker in the world by Thinkers50

"A fresh perspective on rediscovering the art of thinking and bridging philosophy and business; a provocative read for 2017, offering guidance on how to stay ahead of the disruption game."
Whitney Johnson, Thinkers50 Management Thinker, Author of critically-acclaimed *Disrupt Yourself: Putting the Power of Disruptive Innovation to Work*

"A passionate manifesto about our fast-paced world. Anders delivers solutions for the challenges of today and how everyone of us can shape what's coming next."
Professor Sydney Finkelstein, Tuck School of Business at Dartmouth College and bestselling author of *Superbosses*

Published by
LID Publishing Ltd.
The Record Hall, Studio 204,
16-16a Baldwins Gardens,
London EC1N 7RJ, United Kingdom

31 West 34th Street, 8th Floor, Suite 8004,
New York, NY 10001, US

info@lidpublishing.com
www.lidpublishing.com

A member of:

BPR
Business Publishers Roundtable

www.businesspublishersroundtable.com

© Anders Indset 2017
© LID Publishing Ltd. 2017

Printed in Great Britain by TJ International
ISBN: 978-1-911498-23-0

Illustrations by Hana Gärtner

ANDERS **INDSET**

WILD
KNOWLEDGE

OUTTHINK THE REVOLUTION

LONDON   MONTERREY
MADRID   SHANGHAI
MEXICO CITY BOGOTA
NEW YORK   BUENOS AIRES
BARCELONA   SAN FRANCISCO

CONTENTS

CHAPTER IV
VALUES & EMOTIONS   142
- Let's work on education first
- The core of 3:
  Empathy, self-awareness & honesty
- Finding your mantra
- The power of now
- Realism | relationism | the network
- A final secret: share
- The company heart
- Live (love) it or leave it

CHAPTER V
OUTTHINK THE REVOLUTION
A (BUSINESS) PHILOSOPHICAL OUTRO   196
- Practical philosophy
- The world ahead
- A global model

INTRODUCTION

"The leaders of today need the philosophy of the past paired with the scientific knowledge and technology of tomorrow."

Wild knowledge is something real and new, something that no one else has, or has yet put a price on. But once it is documented, replicated and disseminated, it no longer has a price, as technology kicks in and the efficiency game takes over in our zero-cost society.

Capital, or cash, is no longer king because wild knowledge cannot be bought. The unknown unknowns, the recipes we try to explain in retrospect and then copy – this is what we seek. Today, we can ponder what we do not know, what we cannot explain, or what we do not know that we know. Anything else is replicated and produced at zero cost.

For hundreds of thousands of years, nothing really happened. No one took notice of change, simply because it all happened so slowly. First homo erectus, and later homo sapiens, crouched on the ground looking up at the stars, wondering what it was all about.

It wasn't until what we've called the "Age of Enlightenment," with its peak in the 18th Century, that things started to accelerate. We started creating scientific instruments to explore the world around us, and this quest for knowledge has been growing exponentially ever since. Before us lies a journey to upgrade our species with new challenges not only for the business world, but also for us as humble human beings, our society and everything we have built. Today, we've arrived at a place where every aspect of our lives – our moral framework and everything around us – is driven by technology. And that opens our political models and cultural structures to the relentless assault of "disruption".

In this book, I will take a look at how leaders today need to become 'leaders of change', what is needed in our lives and the business world today, both from a leadership and a management perspective. How businesses today need to master "the mind", "the heart" and "the hands" of the organization, the leadership, management and execution. Furthermore, I will look at how we need to apply practical philosophy in order to cope with change and the challenges ahead. There is too much bullshit in business today and it cannot be tolerated. Philosophers are needed to question everything at the scene, and to support solving what used to be abstract questions but have now become questions on the plate that will be solved by new technological progress.

Having established that basis, the purpose of this book is to plot out a core methodology for learning; to devleop the right mindset and map out a landscape where one can in fact find wild knowledge.

Being able to cope with change is key to outthinking any revolutionary disruption and managing in the 21st Century. For business leaders and companies, this means changing twice. Innovation is all about the execution; it is the "action" part. Changing perception, how we see the world, is the second part; it is the core pillar. While one is about action, the other requires thinking. We may try to train ourselves to think creatively, yet so often we fail to understand that the most important part of this is REALLY THINKING.

Our future, however that pans out – any future, for that matter – will not resemble the past. The challenge is to break out of deeply ingrained modes of thinking, or mindsets that deduce how things will be based solely on how things are or were. To challenge this state, of course, requires trust, bravery, failure and risk-taking. Scary stuff, but absolutely critical if we wish to break through to new paradigms, ask new questions and move on to the next chapter in our infinite journey. Those who live between paradigms – who have the capacity to see the unseen, or to grasp the unknown unknowns – find wild knowledge. These are the enlightened individuals we need to learn from, though it's likely many will consider them "crazy".

So, instead of taking a deep dive into the concept of knowledge, this is an attempt to create a basic outline for seeking wild knowledge.

It's a blueprint for creating models and an overall atmosphere – a culture, if you like – where it's possible to find answers to startling new questions that challenge our current understanding of reality.

This exercise is, in the end, about overcoming the complexity and frustration of life in the 21st Century. This book is about getting a better understanding of change, knowledge, ideas, creation, change in perception, feelings and emotions. It is about being a "mensch" – about being human. It is about NOT being a zombie or a robot, but rather recognizing and developing all we have that makes us human. The word mensch refers to being a human being, but in my definition it is much more. It is the opposite of "unmensch" – basically the conscious process of doing right or wrong within your own mental framework. A mensch is therefore not "just" a human being, but a conscious being who chooses right over wrong within his or her own values, moral framework and state of consciousness, on one hand so complex, on the other so simple. It is the void, the "I", the subject. It is you. Understanding this simple difference will help us evolve into something better and give us the capacity to actually enjoy progress and change. Are you being an unmensch or a mensch? It's a simple enough question to ask as we scrutinize our own value systems.

So, this is a new fresh approach to bridge business and philosophy, and apply practical philosophy in these fast-paced times. It is about the feeling you get when looking someone in the eyes during a conversation, about taking time to reflect, about rediscovering "the lost art of thinking". Today, society keeps gathering knowledge faster than it achieves wisdom. Those who succeed are those who manage to find structure and exploit the powers of wild knowledge – the untamed tangle of data, learning and experience that flourishes in our lives and courses through our minds. This is an attempt to open the doors to what we actually know, shed light on the unknown knowns, and uncover all that is left out and lost in our day-to-day rat race. These are the fields we know are important but we cannot grasp; the things that can make a real difference. It is about the here and now.

Today, more than ever, this world of ours needs philosophers. We are living in an incredibly beautiful moment – perhaps the most exciting time yet in the long arc of human history. While we hustle through life searching for our purpose, trying to understand and define the "art of living", we should also try to understand and master the "art of thinking". What is it that makes us human, that distinguishes us from the machines? What is it precisely that makes a mensch?

We read about progress in quantum computing, the road toward singularity and perfect knowledge, but Artificial Intelligence (AI) and robots are not there yet. No, they still have some years (not many though) to reach a state where we will have clarity on where this journey is taking us. We are hoping and waiting for a new paradigm, where new answers will reveal themselves. As we proceed we see that development will not stop, it is infinite, and the speed of development continually increases. We are in a sense at the beginning of infinity, poised for infinite change and infinite knowledge. We should be conscious that we are barreling down the road toward infinity, infinite knowledge and new opportunities… and we should accept this.

Today we are upgrading our lives and the focus is on AI, not my initials, but artificial intelligence. It's not a matter of artificial consciousness or artificial thoughts, but disembodied machine intelligence. Will we merge with technology? Of course we will, to some degree or another. We are making rapid progress in AGI (Artificial General Intelligence, or strong/full AI), the ability of a machine to perform "general intelligent action," or have the intelligence to successfully perform intellectual tasks that a human being can do.

Quantum computers will bring significant societal changes and they might be just around the corner – we are most likely only talking a couple of years. In no time at all, perhaps within the next 15 to 20 years, we will have the opportunity to buy the computing power of a human brain. Look out, 1,500 IQ (and 15,000 IQ!), here we come. We are bio-hacking our way to what we might call "trans-humanism". But there are limits. In the not-too-distant future, there may be trillions of hyper-interdependent computers connected to our species, all 8 billion of us. These technological breakthroughs will be exponential and continuous, but we are talking about computing power and not about being human. It is, after all, consciousness that really makes us human.

The challenge facing today's scientists and futurists is to try to achieve perfect knowledge and post-humanism. The progress of science, and what we decide to do with our newly gained powers and knowledge, will be a reflection of our defining moral framework. Just as we tamed stone, fire and bronze, we also need to find ways to tame the technology we create. I'm confident that we will.

We need the ability to judge which aspects of future knowledge will be applicable to business and to our lives in general. As a starting point, let's establish that a fact (knowledge) is something we build upon to gain wisdom until suddenly there is a new sense of how we perceive the world. With the technology we have available today, and the narcissistic quest for attention we see all around us, we tend to believe and share knowledge that we then build upon. This is not necessarily related to the exponential speed of change, but more because of the limitations on how we think, what we question and our state of consciousness. It's what I call "the art of thinking clearly". With the new media systems we have created, and the inherent reward mechanisms for sharing through them, we find ourselves in an unchallenged state of knowledge. It's a phenomenon I call "vicious wisdom". Vicious wisdom comes from people who are thoroughly convinced about the information they share, and who are celebrated for doing so by their own, self-congratulatory group. This is one of the biggest challenges we face as an interdependent society. We are driven by social media and sucked into a world of opportunities that is constantly moving toward *higher, faster and better*. There may have never been more bare-faced narcissism, yet we have never been more open and social. Technology is going to help us exploit our feelings, and tap into our consciousness. This is one of the biggest challenges we face as an inter-dependent society. We are driven by social media and sucked into a world of opportunities that is constantly moving toward higher, faster and better. There may have never been more bare-faced narcissism, yet we have never ever been deeper into the recesses of our minds.

This book is, I hope, food for thought for frustrated business people who, more than ever, doubt their own knowledge. It's squarely aimed at those who feel like they are standing at the gate, outside the velvet rope, as the rocket's about to take off. I want to encourage the reader to hop on, to take that journey of self discovery. This is not about my journey, but rather yours. I want you to enjoy it, to experience the now, to embrace a life of hyper-curiosity and ongoing learning.

This is a book about how to think differently, how to take control of the chaos, and at the same time expect and accept more chaos. It's about getting your arms around more change, and more turbulent environments (business and otherwise) without letting that upheaval control your life. Chaos and turbulence are not negatives. They can be a force – your force, your strength.

In this book, I will not teach you what to think, or pretend to provide all the answers. Instead, my aim is to influence how you think… to put you in a position to challenge the answers and the status quo, on the road toward mutual goals. Let's create bridges, new views and ever greater possibilities.

This is your exciting journey, where you wander up and down the spectrum of levels of consciousness and exploit the wonderful 'sein' of being a "mensch." This is central to the lost art of philosophy, and how YOU can outthink the revolution.

Røros, January 2017

CHAPTER I
WILD KNOWLEDGE
A (BUSINESS) PHILOSOPHICAL INTRO

WELCOME TO THE NEW WORLD

I am a radical optimist and I believe that only in creative scenarios can you really exploit the potential of "mensch". The creative skills we have today come from devising solutions, making mistakes, and sometimes failing miserably, all of which eventually led to error-corrections for the better. But it really does not matter whether you're an optimist or a pessimist. To hew exclusively to either extreme is a mistake. Still, I consciously choose positivism… and so should you. Anything else will leave you frustrated and you'll spend your life on a rollercoaster ride with far more downs than ups. This is the potential future scenario I want to share my thoughts on and work through with you.

When reading this book, I want you to stop and pause, think and reflect, and go out and do some "thinking out loud". Discuss the topics and raise the questions that pop into your mind with others when you are intrigued or provoked. It is a book where you read a couple of pages, then get into the dialogue you need to clarify your thoughts. Write to me or discuss it with your spouse or a colleague. This will lead to new questions and thoughts, I promise!

"True Wisdom is found in sweet spots hidden in plain sight, between the unconscious state of tamed knowledge and the conscious state of experiences put into place."

Even before Socrates had his dialogues with Plato, the topic of change was on the agenda. Greek philosopher Parmenides suggested that you cannot really change anything, that change is impossible. He was at odds with philosopher Heraclitus of Ephesus, who believed that change was the underlying law of the universe. There is, he asserted, nothing permanent except change (a notion misattributed to many sources).

Heraclitus' 2,500-year-old quotation has never been truer: "No man ever steps in the same river twice, for it's not the same river and he's not the same man." And the word 'change' has been bugging us ever since. Italian diplomat and political theorist Niccolò Machiavelli took it further and laid the groundwork for what we call 'Modern Philosophy' with his book *The Prince*, first published around 1515. Today, 500 years have passed and change is still very much on the agenda.

"Change" remains a vexing problem for every CEO. "CEOs are leaders of change," so welcome to the new world. Another revolution? Another disruption? 2.0., 3.0, 4.0, – GET IT?! All these stupid buzzwords. Change is normal now, everything is changing, and that is what we have in front of us. We know that nothing escapes change. It is not just restricted to IT or technology, but runs through every aspect of our lives.

The good thing... we can still outthink it. And I believe we have to. We need new questions, new models and, as Hollywood's Marty McFly and Doc Brown taught us on October 21st, 2015, we have arrived in the future – there's really no future anymore, it is up to you and me to create and improvise what is to come. Change comes so quickly, progress is so rapid, the flow of information is so unrelenting that anything we might predict for the future is actually a reflection of the present.

"Today, philosophers are needed everywhere, in every industry and in every organization."

What I have learned, for the better or worse, I have learned from philosophy. And I believe that we need to look back to philosophy to create concepts for understanding the world, to introduce groundbreaking work, and to present the world to pioneers in all fields, allowing them to think, research and analyze.

The real change-makers today are not the likes of Google co-founders Sergey Brin and Larry Page; the web's pioneers do not even understand the technology or the true nature of the internet themselves. No one does. It will not be populist movements or leading politicians (politicians are only managers – they cannot lead the change). We are now seeing the emergence of a generation of hackers, and face an evolutionary change in culture and creativity. These swarms of young people are the new powers. And they have only just begun. Never has the gap between the 20-year-olds and 40-year-olds been more expansive. People in their 40s are at times frustrated by the digital world buzzing in their pockets and eating up their time in an age of individualism and the exalted "I". On the other hand, those in their 20s are single di-viduals, primarily living connected lives and using physical space as a secondary playground for participatory cultures, co-creation, creativity, joy and working on the solutions of tomorrow.

Philosophy from the old world might not have kept up with the speed of science and technology, but today, more than ever, we need to combine these fields. We need to rescue blind spots from history, hidden in plain sight, and combine them with the scientific knowledge and technology of tomorrow. Wisdom is not something to have, it is something you forever seek.

Today many hide behind suits and their ties are so tightly bound that they are unable to breathe. Being from the "older generation" in the 21st Century, I understand the pressure to look like you have it all, to exude confidence and competence. We have to look competent or we lose the respect of other people. A manager once told me, "I cannot drop the tie. I will lose my creditability and my people will not trust me." At that point I began to think that the world had become a bit out of control, and we hadn't been very good at correcting the errors in our system. A necktie earns trust? Of course not. Inside of this frustrated, ranting and raving, funky-sock-wearing being is a person trying to find his real, authentic self. He's consumed by a sense of loss of power, because he used to know something no one else knew, and he used to be in control. Although we may understand this behavior, I do not think we should accept it. Now the biggest challenge facing 55-plus male managers is the need to stay curious and learn. Incompetence and lack of knowledge can be a problem, but trust and respect, in the long run, do not come from layering on a tie and a tailor-made suit.

We can be, and do anything that we want to, that is what we are thought by our parents. A terrible free ride into stupidity and misery if anything, but in fact this is where we are. Walt Disney's famous quote "if you can dream you can do it" has now become "if you can do it, you can do it" and we have somewhat lost our dreams and something to believe in. A new challenge for all of us is searching for an identity and a story to clinch on to. But the new world for many is a mere reflection of the past. It means waking up in the same room, putting on the same clothes, driving the same road to the same job, executing the same tasks, fighting to climb the next step up the ladder of materialism. Our days are scheduled – the playfulness and the freedom are gone. Every day means treading the same path until we are someday, inevitably, replaced by our children, who will more than likely travel the same path.

But in the future this will also change. We will not have jobs in the traditional sense. The change will be to a task-focused world, revolving around tasks which will be performed within our team. No top and bottom, but more front and back. You throw something in, you get something out. The societal and occupational structures are changing, and we need to stop thinking about the concept of "having a job".

THINKING
BACKWARDS

"*Life is understood backwards, but must be lived forwards.*"

– Søren Kierkegaard

As a young student of philosophy, I concluded that all thoughts and situations had already been considered and studied to a much greater extent than I would ever manage. Although I have great respect for many of the modern thinkers and philosophers, my approach has not been to aim for academia or to become a professor of philosophy. Instead, I try to bridge the work of these geniuses into today's business world. I strive to project the thoughts of Nietzsche, Kant, Hagel, Marx, La Rochefoucauld and others onto the realities of the 21ˢᵗ Century. This is exciting, this idea of bridging the old world to the new, identifying the sweet spots or taking core learnings from the past and applying them to the here and now. What would these geniuses think if they had our technological understanding, access to digital networks and the cumulative progress of academia and science?

The celebrated thinkers of today emphasize analytics and try to find tangible, fixed answers on a wide range of subjects. However, this represents the upper levels of thinking; it does not take the deep dive that many of the philosophers of the past did. I am not here to judge. However, building on the geniuses of the past – copying and stealing some of their thoughts – sounds like a much more exciting approach to me. Looking back and applying that thinking to a potential future problem puts us in a position where, if we put in the work, we might get all the answers we've been seeking. Or come up with the desperately needed new questions.

Forget what you know and what you want. Only then can you leave room for new models, new ideas and structures – the wildness. If we take a closer look at 'thinking' the first question that pops to my mind is, "Where do thoughts come from?" What are thoughts, really? We think about the world and gather our knowledge. When you think, it's between you and the world, the world and you. It's your own subjective reality that you apply to markets, facts, data, products, services, objects, structures, everything. It is how you understand the world.

When you think, what you are doing in most cases is simplifying. We take the reality in front of us and map it to existing models, structures and boxes in our mind. Everything we have in "reality" is agreed upon stories. These stories do not really exist. They also only work as long as we agree on them or, until someone comes and changes our perception, then new stories are created. The only real thing we have is stuff that can either suffer or love. We also talk about this in metaphorical terms in business and society, but the real suffering and loving can only be done by something of real flesh and blood – from what we call human beings, or a "mensch". When you leave a stadium after having watched a soccer game, you simplify the game because there is nothing standing between the reality of the game you just witnessed and yourself. The striker was good, the referee was bad, and so on. This applies to the personal as well as the business world. It's one presumed reality: all that there is in front of you is data, information and attributes. But when you talk to others, they will have their own simplification. There is no difference in the reality; the difference is in the way each of us views, processes and understands this reality internally, through our individual, unique thought process. So, the art of thinking is like playing a game where we simplify and match or create new models and structures for what we have seen externally. Our subjective world is our playing field; it is where the rules of the game are applied (e.g., thinking it through). Here we outline our tactics and strategies in order to be good, perform well, succeed and master the games of life and business. So the supposed reality is out there, but it never really exists in our minds, and to think about the world we can only simplify and create our own unique, individual mental models. Essentially, everything boils down to an individual's own simplification of reality – a simplification of the world itself.

THE MACHINE AND I

In order to manage in the 21st Century, we not only need to study history and learn from the past but also to think about where we are heading. It is important to understand that we have moved beyond things that we can control. Approximately half of the people in the world have access to the internet, and we have self-driving cars, human-carrying drones and virtually unlimited Information on Demand (IoD). It seems that today, the best way to increase efficiency and productivity is to eliminate the need for people. What is it that we are doing? We are creating God(s), upgrading our species to become a God. We had God as "the creator" in the past, but maybe this was wrong all along. Maybe we are moving towards something of these defined God(s) – we are creating this God in a machine (Deus Ex Machina) where we merge with technology and take on immortality, eternal or at-least controlled happiness and divinity.

Have you ever thought about whether a machine can replace you? For now, let's view this as complementary. "Strong AI is like a cosmic lottery ticket: if we win, we get utopia; if we lose, Skynet substitutes us out of existence. (Watch the *Terminator* movies)." PETER THIEL

Perhaps unintentionally, pioneering computer scientist Alan Turing limited the description of AI when he compared it not to minds or thoughts but instead to the process of rational thinking. Out of this, an idea evolved that thinking was computational, rational, and it followed defined, calculated patterns. Machines can do that; they can follow rules and calculate logical patterns. In fact, they can do it a lot better than we can. The "thoughts" of computers can be defined as rational and logical, with a reason and a structured formality. Humans, on the other hand, think differently. Much like the binary system, neurons in the human brain can either be off (0) or on (1). Still, it's almost as if they can be both 0s and 1s at the same time, and combine in random patterns. It is this space – free association and the drift of thoughts – that I believe reflects the limitations of computing power. It's as though scientists are trying to find a way to replicate the human mind solely by taking a technological approach. Although I do support the progress of technology, at the same time I believe there are other fields that should be considered. Philosophy provides one way to deal with this. It is much more complementary than it is contractionary or competitive.

And so, two questions we seek to answer are: can we build machine replicas of ourselves, and can we turn ourselves into machines? We all seek technological solutions to make our lives better. A life of joy and creativity and creation, that is what we want. No chores, no hassle, no unneeded physical interruptions. But we spend very little time thinking about the consequences of such changes. Are there any limits? How far can we go? I do not think there is a limit, yet I strongly believe that the 'I' – the subject and the consciousness – will escape. Still, we need to understand that even in the "new world" we need structures and frameworks, and moral value systems, to support our progress.

What is knowledge? And why is it wild? What about wisdom and wise people? How and why can wisdom be vicious? I already touched on this topic in the introduction, but we should have a closer look at knowledge, as it's such a beautiful concept to explore.

Today, we push and publish what we think is knowledge without challenging our own reference points and our own frameworks. That is why it goes wild. Seeking social status is more imporant to us than the quest for truth and accuracy, and we seek a plausible explanation in some kind of "rear-view-mirror logic". This misconception is called justificationism. We're challenged by the staggering speed of today's information flow and the fact that we do not understand the concept of change. We have a misconception of knowledge; we like to define an authority against it.

The philosophical search for the meaning and definition of knowledge has been bugging thinkers for thousands of years. Yet once we get closer to a definition, it slips away with counter-arguments and fluctuating definitions. For the reader familiar with the philosophical definition of knowledge, this is not about the limits of knowledge.

It is not a philosophical definition, or a scientific approach to defining knowledge. As I have stated, for me knowledge is the basis, the core, a subjective standpoint that is rooted in our view of reality and understanding of the world. It is what we define as "what we know". We human beings, I believe, are on this planet in search of further information and plausible explanations for our own lives.

To some extent or another we have always lived in an information society, and believed we could gather all available information and "know it all". Back in the 1900s, it took approximately 100 years to double all the information in the world, but by 2020 the sum total of mankind's information will be doubling at a rate of every six hours. A lot of junk, yes, but there always has been. Forget Big Data (how big is it anyway?). We should talk about *the right data* – relevant small data, or whatever. Knowledge is being aware of something and, as described, possessing information. Knowledge is really about facts and ideas that we acquire through study, research, investigation, observation and experience (living with our eyes and ears wide open), through trial & error, stealing and mapping it through our sensory experiences.

Wild knowledge is hiding like a secret, waiting to be discovered. It is a change in perception; it is what you didn't know that you know. It is the "unknown knowns"or even the "unknown unknowns". Only now it is not one long-term challenge; it is multiple (n) challenges. That makes it so exciting and wild. Wild knowledge is what drives us forward, it moves society, and it is what all businesses are looking for so desperately – to adapt and find "new ways of thinking".

With all of the technological and scientific progress today, we are rapidly organizing our knowledge. This is actually what science is, organized knowledge. Wisdom, on the other hand, maps to what you have learned for yourself. Wisdom is organized life, and where knowledge speaks, wisdom listens. Wisdom is the ability to discern and judge which aspects of knowledge are true, lasting, right, and if they are applicable to your (organized) life.

We tend to take what we know (or what we think we know) very seriously, and this is a problem. There are many approaches to describing wisdom, and some might claim that wisdom cannot be vicious. But a more cautious philosophical approach tells us that wisdom can be vicious. Vicious wisdom comes from claiming that you are wise. It is the trap of *Wise-Doom*. To quote Shakespeare, "The fool don't think he is wise, but the wise man knows himself to be a fool." In other words, wisdom is not something you have, but something you seek. And if you believe you have it, beware, lest it becomes vicious and capable of destroying you at any moment.

There is nothing wrong with confidence in one's own wisdom, knowledge and skills. However, over-confidence leaves us blind and gets us into trouble. We all know that we are above average. When we are asked about our driving skills, we rate ourselves as above average and less likely to cause an accident. The same goes for doctors and professors... and in fact, the higher you climb, it seems the bias of overestimating becomes increasingly evident. And with this blindness, many of these professions become increasingly vulnerable to replacement by the technology and advanced capabilities of robotics.

We think knowledge is a shortcut to glory, a wonderful thing, stable and achievable, and close – if we only put in a bit of effort. It will give us all we've imagined: the confidence, the monitary benefits, a successful life. But once we achieve those cursory goals, we will find that there is much more. The more we gain, the more we become aware of how little we know – which is actually a state of frustration.

Tamed knowledge is replaceable. Wild knowledge implies that the more tamed knowledge we have, the more we'll be limited in our ability to unlearn and unthink. Having the ability to unlearn and unthink, together with a touch of playfulness, are what we need to think like a beginner and come up with new solutions and ideas.

One thing about knowledge is that we want to aquire it and think about reaching an end state. The end is the goal, but the wildness and deeper understanding of knowledge are hidden in the blind spots. True success is found in the blind spots, between the unconscious state of knowledge and the conscious state of wisdom.

There are some things in our practical experience and theoretical knowledge that are difficult to explain. Searching for the next big thing can come from creating so-called temporary monopolies. And yes, the future will be created and invented; the question is by whom.

In these times of uncertainty, chaos and volatility, if you try to control knowledge and the uncontrollable, you will go insane, as packed/controlled knowledge will be something found in the machine, the algorithms, and here we can simply not compete. You, as a "Mensch", can either sit back and drift (or be dragged) into life, or take control of the 'now' and proactively chart a course of progress, creation and change.

All thought, I clearly share the views of the ancient Greek philosopher Heraclitus that the only constant we have is change – still, whether nothing changes or everything changes remains somewhat a philosophical question, but the conscious "I" is the only thing that can take control. Are you ready?

CHAPTER II
IDEAS &
MAGIC

*"Your next Idea
will eventually
replace your
old business
model."*

Where do ideas come from? What about creativity? What are companies actually searching for when they look for innovative people? In the 21st Century we are obsessed with finding creativity, ideas and the next big thing – the wild knowledge – because, at least from a business standpoint, progress is all we have. Ideas are at first wild… and then we try to put them into boxes based on our mental models and experiences.

But ideas have never been logical. It was never like that with the statue of David, the Mona Lisa, Beethoven's 5th. These masterworks weren't created out of a strategic plan and logical steps, but rather through a number of subsequent trials and failures. Ideas arise out of ignition, stealing & copying, a forced coincidence, destruction of old mental models and frameworks. *One* universal recipe? FORGET IT – not with ideas. These ideas did not occur out of nowhere, nor were they quickly churned out by someone called "the artist". These masterpieces are only an abstraction of the total effort – the rigorous experiments, the process of trial and error, revision and discovery. We tend to blend together and mix up these terminologies, and we're likely to do that with innovation and creativity. But as we take a closer look, we discover that they are not the same.

The whole process of idea generation is perhaps best described by Ed Catmull, CEO of film animation studio Pixar, Inc. His company, which has turned out blockbuster after blockbuster, is truly a place where ideas come alive. What is the genius machinery behind this company, one might ask, and has it always been like that? Catmull describes, in one of the greatest books on the topic, *Creativity Inc.*, how the whole idea driving Pixar is to move from "Suck" to "Non-Suck" through a journey of discoveries. Throughout recent history, the number of tries before finding the perfect storyboard has increased at Pixar, meaning many more sucks before reaching the desired non-suck stage. For the movie "A Bug's Life" they had 27 storyboards; "Finding Nemo" had 43; a couple of years later "Ratatouille" needed 69; "wall-E" needed 98 and some 125,000 drafts.

In order to succeed in such a working mode, you need freedom to exploit. You need to be able to basically fail that many times before you reach the end product. But for Pixar, it is failing within a comfort zone. There are places where you are allowed to fail. Successful companies have that openness within the organization, without judging and making it a matter of ego. Pixar has introduced something called "Plussing", where a group is shown the storyboard and asked to judge it based on ways that it can be done even better. For instance, "I like the hair or the ears," or, "What you did there was great, but what do you think about making it even longer?" This culture of working with ideas has established Pixar as one of the most admired brands of recent times, with tremendous financial success. The movie "Cars" generated $10 billion (yes billion) in revenue from merchandising alone.

Companies such as Pixar are not common, and there have been many unsuccessful attempts to create standardized operating models. But the desired "process" of creation is doomed to fail from the start by using the disjunctive terminologies of ideas, creativity and innovation in a blended mix. An innovative company is one that can change and adapt within its own business segment. It is one that can master change within its playing field, and come up with new ways to do things in better, more efficient ways. Change in this way is what we call horizontal change. Creativity, on the other hand, is more often radical. It involves a change in perception and viewpoint – creating something from an existing product by seeing it from a completely new angle, with new technologies and new methods.

As I mentioned in the beginning, cash is not king anymore. It is, if anything, a strong number two. Wild knowledge is in the driver's seat now. It is the power of ideas, the force of injecting a new perception into our lives and minds. It's the good idea, the change that makes a difference. Wild knowledge is what everyone is looking for today. Yet, the big questions – "Where does it come from?" "Where do you find it?" – remain unresolved.

What can we do to move closer to finding new ideas? On the one hand, we can talk and write about it. But theoretical musings, and the limitations of our powers of expression, actually dilute what it's really all about. In the final analysis, ideas are about creation, about actually doing stuff.

Where DO good ideas come from? The paradox we are faced with today is that, with the rapid progress of science and technology, companies are struggling as never before to find new innovation drivers. At times, it feels like all ideas must be big, extreme. At the same time, the gap between commodities, known facts and the things we (most likely) will never be able to figure out is increasing. The hidden secrets that we can discover are, for most of us, now in view: mysteries like the endless universe and unlimited galaxies, the concept of a God or the consciousness of human beings. But is that how it really is? Scientists believe we can find the answers, discover how the mind works, and create robots that can take care of everything. However, our strange mind does not necessarily agree or see how we can tame innovation. So it remains wild and the search continuous.

In today's business world, when organizations are on to something and hitting home runs (being successful), this is when ideas are needed the most – to keep them from being run over by the tidal wave of *the next big thing*. We talk about disruption, and about change, but having your ideas in place puts you in a position to renew yourself and keep ahead of the herd.

We think of creativity and ideas as mysterious, but I have learned one thing over the years – progress and creation come out of DOING STUFF. Putting different minds together and just STARTING – reveling in a fruit ball of various creatures, a fun park of joy, if you like. We try to force our ideas through models and methodologies, but what creative people do is combine other ideas with their own, copying and stealing from geniuses of the past. These ideas come to life in spaces where we are allowed to be weird, where we can screw up, where we can probe and improve and make new discoveries. The breakthrough ideas and the special moments are driven by serendipity and are led by dreams and passionate people trying to create change to make an impact. They set out on one journey and go through moments of creation, accompanied by periods of frustration. Like writing a book, it is all about doing. Making the first crappy draft, and then the second less-crappy draft… until you finally say, "This is it."

Change in a business comes through using an ongoing process, executed by a team that continuously moves, with the requisite time, mindset and flow, to continuously create. As we continue to move, our universe is expanding with ever-increasing speed, and it only goes forward. The beauty of this is that if you can also reflect, think and use individual powers to actually create something new, something outside of your borders and frameworks, and tap into your potential, then chances are you will enjoy the journey.

Ideas and progress are not found within the borders. Change will not come out of like-minded consultants, who are the same age, gender and heritage, all from the same business schools. To achieve change you need more chaos, not less.

The progress will come from leaders, thinkers and fruit-cases. We will now take a closer look at how to find wild knowledge and the mysteries and magic around "IDEAS".

Ideas are created; they are not given to you. To generate ideas, you have to start "doing." And with that, basically, this chapter should come to end. It's as simple as that.

Too many people talk about all the things they thought about doing or should have, might have, could have done ('schmould' have). I've met many people who carry around what they believe is a great idea, but they've never gotten past the social bragging stage – simply talking about it at a local bar. Be sure of one thing: ideas are not born "great". (PERIOD!)

So there are talkers and there are "doers". Ideas arise when you do stuff, when you try stuff out, when you don't limit yourself and when you are not afraid to be bold. No stage is big enough not to fail. But that said, a comfort zone, a secure place where you can be probed, is in fact highly recommended. It is when you can change your perception, where you can be open to entering a totally and radically new way of seeing your own world. It is here that you can tame the wild knowledge. So, reinvent yourself and leave your comfort zone. Ideas are imperfect; disruption and change are led by those challenging the status quo and questioning the known facts (the tamed knowledge). Is there one indisputable formula for success? Sure, some people have biological advantages in that they are simply "born creative". Those lucky few have a head start, but is that all it takes? No… many great companies, successful entrepreneurs, renowned artists and famous athletes have come out of the crucible of *doing and trying*. The great Wayne Gretzky and "His Airness" Michael Jordan are both legends in their respective sports, ice hockey and basketball. They each have had their individual journeys and have grown out of just doing, taking the shot, trying. As Gretzky said, "You miss all the shots you don't take."

As far as we know there is no academic key to creativity, disruptive thinking or changing one's perception. Change in perception can be found through philosophy, art, science or political theory, between the conscious and unconscious state, between structured methodology and wild chaos or in the art of playfulness. However, the perfect mixture, the usage, the recapture and the reconfiguration of knowledge makes it so special that, even though we are not aware of it, it is wild and it can strike at any moment.

So what are ideas then? First of all, ideas are neither true nor false; they exist only in the mind. For example, someone may have an idea of God but it would be wrong to say that this idea of God is false or true. An idea is simply what I am thinking about, not a factual statement. Ideas can then be scientifically or technologically proven or debunked, or one can set about finding answers and solutions based on the idea.

We relate ideas to creativity, to innovation and to thinking. Thinking and ideas paired with your experience lead to new knowledge, something that you now know. You take the knowledge and build wisdom. The opposite of wisdom is not lack of wisdom, it is *vicious wisdom*. When we talk about wisdom based on knowledge (and yes, there are other ways to interpret this concept), we expect a certain result based on outcomes we have experienced in the past. For example, we might expect value. Children, on the other hand, have fresh, limitless ideas because they do not know the value. Therefore, they cannot expect the result.

Businesses need both innovation and creativity, and you need to ignite both. Innovation is your, or a company's, capacity to change the presumed reality – by launching new products, for example. Alternately, creativity is the ability to change perception or make someone else experience a new point of view. Both terminologies belong to "change", which has become a bit of a 21st Century buzzword. So, while creativity is about ideas, innovation is about bringing ideas into action, through strategy, process, budget, teamwork, etc. Creativity needs thinking, and innovation needs action. And yes, you can have innovation without creativity, and creativity can flourish without innovation.

We just need to start exploiting ideas, however complex they may be. It's helpful to look at recent "breakthroughs," where doing stuff – just starting – ignited a big change. These are what we in retrospect define as genius ideas or game-changing innovations, and they invariably came from the "starters". We now see Spotify and Apple leading the way in things that were first considered to be impossible, but they all root back to the igniters of disruption and their unorthodox, creative ideas. Those who challenged the status quo, the ones who said NO! They are the trailblazers who endured the resistance and understood that there were no straight lines, no recipes, no limits to what or how. Napster, Pirate Bay, Uber, Bitcoin – these were all illegal at first, but each went on to cause the big changes that we are seeing today. These hackers are driving the change (#hackersoftheworldunite). They are the real change makers.

Our egos can to be blame for struggles with getting started and generating creative new ideas. As soon as we "get going" we immediately want to be "professionals," to be seen as experts on something or another. It is what is expected of us, what we believe is important, how we've been conditioned to think. There is nothing wrong with making progress and being successful, but we will be in a much better place if we can remain amateurs at heart and think like beginners. This was also something Apple founder Steve Jobs referred to in his famous Stanford University graduation speech in 2005, where he said, "Stay Hungry-Stay Foolish." Have fun, stay curious. If you try to control everything, "to be an expert," then you will fail and hit the ground like a rock. If you are an expert, then you may think that you know a lot. If you have "finished learning," then you have only *finished*, and it is highly likely that you have not learned a lot. Think and act like an amateur, a concept described by Danish talent and high-performance anthropologist Rasmus Ankersen, who refers to himself as "a professional amateur" in his books, *The Gold Mind Effect* and *Hunger in Paradise*. Be sure to stay an amateur, and eventually doors of creativity will open. In companies, we call this "keeping an entrepreneurial mindset."

It is common for big corporations to look within, to try to train current employees how to "think like a start-up." Start-ups are admired for their innovative, disruptive and co-creative nature. But we need to remember that start-ups fail too. You want to build an organization with a changed mindset, one that can accept differing views and adopt a different perception. The secret is to remain an amateur, because experts are limited by their expertise. We do not even know what we actually know but by remaining an amateur you are kept on your toes and keep moving, and chances are you will get somewhere special.

"The beginner sees the possibilities, the expert all the limitations."

There are a lot of things I like about the term "entrepreneur" and, when picking investments or assessing young people, the expression embodies much of what we look for; the means, the purpose, the human capital. But, beyond the standard definition, we need people who get off dead-center and just start to do stuff – the *igniters*. There is too much emphasis on the buzzword "start-ups". Young entrepreneurs need to operate in a mode where they can focus on the future and have a vision – not seek the first possible exit or do anything that can make money. We need to work on changing our perception and move into a state of "STARTING". We need to find people with different mindsets, those who can help us adopt novel viewpoints and think of new ideas for our business. Gone are the days of the strong individuals who could single-handedly halt change and revolution. Instead, "the world" is driving us, and we need to be open to change, though we should not be driven by the forces of change.

For some "starters" or "igniters", there might also be other challenges, of course. For many, the difficulty is not necessarily in finding new ideas, but in letting go of the old ones. Instead of adding complexity, it is all about a mindset of simplifying. To reflect on how to let go, and how to simplify… that is our challenge. Having said that, the biggest failure is still that many people just don't get started. Progress is the result of the small steps you take, by putting one foot in front of the other, and launching into a journey. Along the way, many falter because they see the road ahead as too long and too rocky. They're hobbled by their calcified perception of how it is, or how it will be. It is by showing up, executing, and taking action every day that these "breakthrough ideas", "breakthrough technologies" and "eureka moments" are written into stories and celebrated as something unique. It is often the case that you do not just start once; you have to come back and start over, and over, and over, and over, and over again.

So when making a start, can you just copy older recipes for success? Yes, yet you cannot endlessly mimic the patterns and personal dynamics of someone else. No, you need to be aware of how your mindset can be changed. One of the most crucial mistakes that we make is to believe that we will be better off if we just have more information. But actually, it is what we don't know that can help us, the unknown unknowns or the unknown knowns that we can tap into. From the outside it always seems like chaos, but progress is in fact just that: chaotic. Our job is to tame it and look for the wildness, pairing new technology with new mental models and views to create something new. This is the wild knowledge we are looking for.

Ideas often evolve from a shared context of learning. In the beginning, these ideas are not good; in fact, no idea starts out being good. Think about the first car, plane, mobile phone or computer. The "starting point" can and should be informal; it should be a space where you consciously discover, jointly learning and exploiting open and casual dialogue rather than sticking to stiff agendas. Expecting perfection at first will kill off the idea before you even get started. The start is best achieved by having multiple views. Starting alone, starting with a diverse group of people, starting over again – the crucial part is that you have a start to focus on and build upon. Only then can you break out of existing rules, shatter outdated stereotypes and exploit the power of imagination. Looking at competitors or even seeking competitive environments can also be great place to start – as igniters do. The Darwinist "survival of the fittest" – the speed and success of adaptation to new environments – is often a true starting point for creation. Having many ideas, and exploiting various options and thoughts, has been a successful creativity driver throughout history. History shows us that even some of the brightest minds had thousands of ideas and labored in the messy churn of trial and error mode.

If you are looking for new (breakthrough) ideas or ways to "start" a successful business, then you should go for vertical change, search for economies of scale, look for proprietary technologies and networks. Horizontal change is simple. You copy things that work and improve upon them to make them more efficient or consumable. These slight variations will not help you in the long run unless you already have a strong brand or you can build one, although they may represent a chance to add media value to your offering. Without this, horizontal change becomes nothing more than a pricing game. Vertical change, on the other hand, means creating something totally new. In their initial business plans and designs, entrepreneurs starting from scratch should aim for something that has potential for great scale – something as simple as the factors that drove the success of Google. Before Google, search engines basically ran a portal that required users to make many page impressions, and they would keep people on the site for as long as possible. The business strategy was, "If I can keep visitors on the page, I am successful and can make money." Google, however, had the idea that users should leave the search site as quickly as possible, because they had found what they were looking for, and they would happily return the next time.

On the journey of creation, you are bound to encounter enemies – people constantly telling you that what you set out to do is simply not doable. But one of the great philosophers on the topic, Immanuel Kant, in his essay, *What is Enlightenment: An Answer to the Question*, cites the Latin motto 'Sapere aude' (Always be Wise). "Have courage," he said, "to use your own reason!" That is the story of every person who has ever created something special. It is like ripping apart a perfect picture in an imperfect world.

If we define great ideas as success, then it is easy to see that they always go hand-in-hand with failure. One cannot live without the other. If there is not failure, there will not be creation or radical progress. In the process toward success there will be jealousy, and there will be struggles and fights against structures. Then, there will be "eureka" moments, cheers and admiration. When creating, be sure to keep the mind clear, and as you bump up against challenges you should pause and go back to the ignition stage. Start again, over and over *again*... and yet again if you have to.

So whatever your understanding of the topic, whether it's thinking, creating, exploiting or trying, it all comes down to STARTING. Have you started yet?

COPY & STEAL

"*Great artists steal and copy with great abandon.*"

In this chapter we will talk about openness and honesty… a perfect counterpoint to copy & steal, don't you think? This is about how you should stop trying to be so "goddamn important" – stop trying to hold yourself to the lofty ideals of self-styled geniuses. Forget it, don't give a ****, you aren't that big of an expert, just accept it. Most of the brainstorms that you think you came up with and brag about actually have their origins elsewhere. Instead of focusing on the party, we should enjoy the progress and the creation. We should look at what we are really doing. Openness, honesty, copycats and stealing, stirred together in the same mix? Have I got you thoroughly confused?

Thinkers such as Aristotle, Plato and Augustinus of Hippo might have created the linguistic and conceptual terminology that enable us to create and invent thoughts, metaphors and artistic uniqueness. But there was already a history of collaborative approaches and the adaptation of ideas from previous thinkers. If these guys have been recognized down through the ages for their brilliant assertions and breakthrough thinking, were they also copying, adapting – some would say "stealing" – from others?

The venerable Walt Disney Company took inspiration for its logo, and the story of Cinderella, from the castle of Neuschwanstein in Germany. The castle logo has become a Disney's trademark and contributed to the company's early success. As for the castle in Neuschwanstein, every year, 1.5 million tourists visit the landmark in southern Bavaria, which was built for King Ludwig II. Although the logo is not an identical representation of the castle, it epitomizes the concept of copying the ideas of others, of other industries and mindsets, and pairing them with our own ideas and creativity. In this case, it was a clear win-win for both Disney and Bavarian tourism.

Perhaps we've been reluctant to use the term "STEAL" when referring to creation and ideas. The Merriam-Webster dictionary defines the word "steal" as to wrongly take and use another person's property, idea, words, etc. Interestingly, though, the word "wrongly" is not defined. In our minds, and in relation to ideas and creativity, the notion of stealing suggests the need for exclusivity. This concept was best described in the book *Karaoke Capitalism*, by Swedish management thought leaders Jonas Ridderstraale and Kjell Nordström. More recently, it was explored in the book *Missfit Economy*, by Alexa Clay. But if we take a closer look, and zero-in on the word "wrongly", what is it that's actually wrong about stealing ideas? If we think about it, most achievements are exactly that – copying someone else, adapting their material with our own unique flair, creating an individual interpretation of something that was already there. We see this in today's popular TV talent shows, such as "The Voice", which feature artists who perform well-known songs with a personal flair. In the final analysis, they copy ("steal") the abstraction and simplification of a creative process initiated by someone else. These casting shows simplify things by giving the work's original "owner" or "author" recognition and praise. In other fields, however, the recognition gets lost, so the same act is seen as a clear-cut case of wrongly using someone else's idea. As with ideas in other fields, the crucial part is, of course, the passion, the training and the talent. But recognizing and celebrating the originator is, in a sense, a ploy to get away with stealing. In the business world, this can only be respectably pulled off by becoming more open and honest about how we achieve something "new" or how we make progress. There is nothing wrong with capitalizing on new packaging and positioning a brand. But when creatively exploiting ideas in the business world, one cannot proclaim, "I am an expert – a veritable genius! – and I came up with everything myself."

Can we, and should we, talk about stealing? Yes, because this is actually what we all do, and we might as well be open about it. Great artists steal and copy with great abandon... but if the essence of your artwork is appropriated, you should give credit to the inspirational originators. Most artists and musicians get their inspiration in more or less the same way, and this is where the business world can learn and adapt, and become better at seeking and taming wild knowledge.

Forget about "Eureka moments".

But doesn't it all need to be something new? No. In fact, we hardly create new stuff at all. What we have been doing is basically improving upon the old stuff. Innovation is not developing the new, but rather bringing ideas into action. In today's fast-paced world you can succeed by focusing on things that have already been said and created, even if merely through repetition. You can in fact become successful by adding a dash of "your own flair".

In an interview in 1994, when talking about the creation of the Macintosh, Steve Jobs explained that it all came down to trying to expose yourself to the best things that humans have ever done, bringing those things together, and then connecting them back to what you are doing. Jobs mentioned Picasso's famous quote on how "good artists copy and great artists steal," and how he had always been shameless about stealing great ideas. Jobs believed that the initial Macintosh was so successful because the people who worked on it were musicians, poets, artists, zoologists and historians who also happened to be the best computer scientists in the world.

We need to accept that this is how it works in the 21st Century. Even at larger corporations, you see this all the time. Steal, catch-up, and then try to adapt and customize and lead the way. In the "winner takes all" marketplace, we should create a working environment where we can play with other people's thoughts and ideas without being judged. This is now seen as "open source", so let's be open and honest about it – we all do it so we should stop pretending otherwise. Trying to claim something as "our idea" or "our thoughts" is really a lie. We look at the ideas and thoughts of others every day, and adapt them as our own. IF in this process there would be something that NO ONE in the world has ever thought of (unlikely for most of us), then feel free to call it innovation, patent it, create your monopoly, and celebrate world domination.

The process of idea generation and creation should not be about our EGO; it should be about progress. And, as we've said, it is important to give credit where credit is due. By celebrating the originator, not yourself, you will do well.

SERENDIPITY

"When your idea is mature, buckle up and take off..."

The challenge with serendipity is that once it strikes – and this is particularly true with an idea – we embrace the new view as a given fact. The challenge becomes managing a real change in perception, which can open the door to something groundbreaking. The key is to probe assumptions and ideas rather than taking them for granted, since we never know when a serendipitous flash of brilliance will occur. We can try to see the change coming, and then try to explain it and see some logic in it (this is what human beings are meant to be good at). But no, that's not likely to happen. There are so many things that have no underlying purpose or no logical explanation other than: You started with "A", then did "B", then all of a sudden moved to "G" and landed on "M". They are just the result of unlikely events or coincidences... of serendipity. I am a firm believer in serendipity. This loaded term, since it was voted one of the ten most difficult words to translate from English in 2004, has been adapted to many languages. This word that is defined as "fortunate happenstance" just has so much magic to it.

One example of how successful people have defined their forced luck – or fortunate happenstance – is the story of the South African golfer who, after hitting a shot that was called lucky, responded: "The more I practise, the luckier I get." Putting in hard work and practice is necessary, though it seems that these "doers" also find serendipity in searching for these wild occurrences.

The whole concept is underestimated, with people talking about what they want to do, or unconscious floaters carrying their dreams around. When it comes to business – and with regard to finding "hidden secrets" and those special ideas (or the wild knowledge) – you can only be successful by going after it. If you look back on your life and career, you will see that countless small things have cumulatively led to significant changes. In many ways, these may not always have been conscious moves, but often the outcome was totally different from what you first anticipated. In today's world, it is almost certain that if you set out to achieve something in two years, you will end up somewhere totally different. In hindsight, we can always come up with a plausible explanation for why things happened. Skill is often just showing up (or starting) combined with something totally different – LUCK, or serendipity. So, serendipity, combined with timing, is in fact forced luck. We must go out and challenge ourselves for things to happen, to force luck. The secret behind many celebrated inventors, artists and geniuses is that they positioned themselves in the right place at the right time. We just have to go out and do it, and beautiful things will happen!

So, the next question is, "Does success come from luck or skill?" In his book *Outliers*, pop-sociologist Malcolm Gladwell asserts that success results from a "patchwork of lucky breaks and arbitrary advantages". Investment guru Warren Buffet famously considers himself a "member of the lucky sperm club" and a winner of the "ovarian lottery". Amazon.com chief Jeff Bezos attributes his company's success to an "incredible planetary alignment" and jokes that his career was the result of "half luck, half good timing, and the rest brains." Microsoft's Bill Gates simply says he "was lucky to be born with certain skills." These geniuses are humble about what they have achieved. In Germany, this idea is described with a beautiful word: "Bodenständigcit". Yet still there are quite a few things to understand about serendipity.

So, what is having luck all about? Was Facebook founder Marc Zuckerberg lucky to get his first investment at the right time? Facebook was not the most advanced web portal at that time, and it wasn't a sure bet functionally or from a branding perspective. Bill Gross, founder of Idealab and numerous other start-ups, got curious about why some companies succeeded whilst others failed. He went out and gathered data and ranked each company on five key factors: the idea; the team/execution; the business model; the funding; and the timing. He looked at 100 companies that he had been involved with at Idealab, as well as an additional 100 companies, and mapped the numbers. His findings were surprising. The most important of his five metrics was timing – 42% of the companies that found success did so because of ideal timing. This teaches us that businesses have to be aware of what customers are really ready for, and what they demand. This can be understood, analyzed and tested. On many occasions this is what we also understand to be "forced luck", or serendipity.

On 14 December, 1911, one of my great countrymen, explorer Roald Amundsen, was the first to reach the South Pole. He wrote, "Victory awaits him who has everything in order – luck, people call it." Several others went on to complete this journey, but Amundsen was the first, and that will forever remain his achievement. He put himself in the right place at the right time and succeeded in a difficult, adventurous undertaking. Some years later, in 1928, scientist Alexander Fleming found that a mysterious antibacterial fungus had grown in a petri dish that he'd forgotten to cover in his laboratory overnight. By accident (or luck) Fleming discovered penicillin, and in 1945 he was awarded with the Nobel Prize for this discovery. So, when we talk about serendipity, it does not mean you should go out and expect the randomness of luck. Rather, you need to put yourself in a position to be able to get it.

Luck resulted in the invention of the Post-it Note by 3M Corp. scientist Spencer Silver, following a screw-up in the lab. He was attempting to create a super-strong adhesive for the aerospace industry, in 1968, but the glue he formulated was in fact incredibly weak. This was followed up by a serendipitous moment years later. Chemical engineer Art Fry suggested using this weak, pressure-sensitive adhesive on the back of paper, allowing it to be stuck to, and easily removed from, virtually any surface. It took another four years before 3M started to test these "stickies" in the marketplace, after they'd become popular within the company.

So, following the first chapters in this section, you can see where this is going. You are in the same position. It is all there for you to grab. When was the last time you tried something new? Go ahead... try something that you are afraid of or have been wanting to try for a long time. NOW is the right time. You should go after serendipity at every opportunity. Exploiting serendipitous discovery is not something for the "chosen ones" or the "special few". Starting and finding wild knowledge and getting tail-winded by serendipity is something YOU CAN DO.

Next, let's look at some of the things you should avoid. But please, do yourself a favour – once have you finished reading for the day, go out and *try something*!

THANKS!

MODELS, METHODOLOGIES & FAILURES

DE CREATIVE

RF GPFATJVF

I love IDEAS. I love creativity. But romanticizing this as a universal key to success would be an unjustified simplification, not applicable for all. Forced luck (serendipity) might not always strike to the extent imagined or required. Working with hundreds of entrepreneurs over the years, I have identified many valuable lessons on finding links between mindset, an atmosphere conducive to creation, and the right mode of execution. In this chapter, we will take a look at the things that can lead to ideas. We'll also take a deeper look at preconceived notions that can distract us on our search for wild knowledge, and might prevent us from discovering and creating new ideas. There are many books written on how to succeed and why some businesses fail. But in this chapter I want to share my own personal learning in this field, and offer some basic pointers that I employ when investing and engaging with companies on models and methodology failures. It is not a chapter about philosophy, nor a deeper reflection on our mind and consciousness. Instead, it is a more practical approach, with thoughts and tips on how we can avoid common pitfalls by learning on this journey of craziness, creativity and wild knowledge.

A very common mistake is that we tend to hold on to old structures and methodologies. Although stability is necessary, we must cultivate doubt and have trust in the uncertain. Often, if you are certain of an outcome, then it is likely that you will screw it up. This is basically what makes scientists and creatives so different. Failures are the beauty of creation. You can always turn it upside down and say many people don't fail – which is true, but for most of us it is all about failure. To quote management thinker and bestselling author Tom Peters, "If you try a lot of things, one might work."

Failure and ideas arising out of trying things is something artists, athletes and inventors have written hundreds of books about. Yet, we still do not understand that if we're feverishly focused on avoiding failure, we will also avoid success. This is basically what Peters said about trying lots of things. In order to increase your success rate, you should go for *more* mistakes. History's most admired inventors, with their thousands of mistakes and failures, teach us that the great ideas always compensate for all the stupid mistakes that paved the way there. It sounds like such a simple model, but it works.

Companies must embrace cultures that allow employees to make mistakes. Instead of focusing on trying to replicate luck (it is a difficult thing to replicate), companies should accept that not every idea will lead to immediate success. This may seem really obvious, yet this mentality is still entrenched in many organizations. I sat down with author Sarah Miller Caldicott, great grandniece of Thomas Edison (who as we know gave birth to the light bulb and many other great inventions), to discuss this. We began by looking at how Edison labored through exhaustive iterations with his team. Sarah explained that her great grandfather's brother was an old hand at making mistakes. She credited him with saying, "I am a master of making mistakes, then I patent them."

The reality of "trial and error" is that some go up and stay up. Most businesses that remain in operation over a longer time go up and come back down, learn from the experience and go on up again. Others hustle at the bottom until finding a way back up. No one wants to make repeated mistakes, and to avoid doing so we try to control everything by finding models to circumvent failure. But when it comes to ideas, there are no models that work for all. Idea-generation and creation are more like alchemy than science. If there was an indisputable, clear-cut formula, everyone would follow it.

BUSINESS MODEL FAILURE

Within the field of entrepreneurship in particular there has always been a great emphasis on business plans. In these volatile and uncertain times, the plan usually is there to show lofty dreams to impress investors. Though it is important to have a guiding path, values and principles, as well as goals to reach, we are now seeing a sharper focus on solving problems and making life easier. There's been a distinct shift toward a problem-solving mentality as opposed to a strict *business plan* view. Why? Because the wild knowledge that businesses are searching for is hidden and cannot be outlined in a plan.

Another thing I have seen over the years is the problem of choosing the wrong business model, or not understanding the implications of one's current business model. Both can put you on the road to failure. There are obviously many reasons why a business can fail, and the planning part is an important factor. Many believe that business plans are created only to convince someone that there is a plan. But I believe that when done correctly, a plan helps to navigate and provides a framework to work within. It is commonly accepted that many quit just before a big breakthrough because they do not see it coming. So, being persistent and sticking with a plan is something that will pay off as long as there is a focus on humanistic capitalism and not just on cash and the ego.

ARE YOU SOLVING REAL CUSTOMER NEEDS?

There are some basic questions everyone should think about when looking for new ideas. You may think that you have all the answers and plenty of great ideas, but taking an external, outside-in approach – listening to and truly understanding the customer – is where you should start. Your products or solutions must solve a real customer problem or add real value. Ask yourself, "What do we do better than anyone else?" "What are my value propositions?" "How are we making our customers' lives better?" Chances are that if you can answer these questions – and have an answer to, "Why will I still be in business in 10 years?" – then you have a better shot at surviving, thriving and truly succeeding.

ARE YOU EXECUTING OPERATIONAL EXCELLENCE?

Many start-ups and businesses fail due to lack of execution. Execution flows from a permanent optimization of decision-making processes. If those are not in place, you will fail. You should put your organization into continuous "light war" mode while trying to act like Robin Hood. Do, Do, Do… except don't focus on what is, but on how you want to be. Setting goals, tracking your progress and molding the organization into a motivated, forward-moving culture of change is crucial.

HAVE YOU CHALLENGED YOUR OWN BUSINESS MODEL?

Another problem is having a fallacious business model, which the founders and owners do not see. Maybe you have underestimated or miscalculated parameters such as the cost of acquiring customers

(CAC) in comparison to customer lifetime value (CLV). Or you are reliant on a technology that is already progressing through new fields. This is difficult to plan for; the best advice is to gather and share your thoughts with people smarter than yourself. Challenge your thoughts or seek environments where you can get external – and, most of all, uncommitted – feedback. Seek feedback from people who have no stake in the answers they provide; they will not want to make themselves or you look good, but rather give you real and honest answers. Don't be afraid to open up and get external advice. Today the real power comes out of groups and networks, not from individuals.

BE AWARE OF EXTERNAL INFLUENCES

There are always external threats to be aware of, legal changes or maybe competitors offering the same value propositions at lower costs. Or, they might have better technology. It is hard to prepare for such threats, but all businesses, and start-ups in particular, should be aware of these potential obstacles.

It is also extremely advisable for businesses to follow tight deadlines. If you have a fixed rollout date, everything else kind of falls into place. When Steve Jobs wanted to create the iPhone, he outlined the features and a set launch date; the rest is history.

It all boils down to whether or not you can define your top priority. Knowing what the most important thing is puts everything else into context, allowing you to align all other activities. If you do not know your top priority and your activities are not aligned with it, there's a problem. Working on multiple priorities slows things down because energy gets sucked out of the organization and its employees. Just like with everything else, we need to challenge our own biases and prepare. Having various methodologies is crucial, but you inevitably will focus on what works for you and your environment.

So what do we mean by model and methodology failure? Even when it is evident that old models are broken, we still use them to explain new things. And that inevitably gets us into problematic situations. We need new ideas, new ways to adapt our models. We live in a new time but are stuck with old structures. Philosophy teaches us to clearly define our thoughts, while at an ever-increasing speed science teaches us how to explain the old in a way that we can understand, or in a new way that we have not been able to see before. These ideas, however, are not the drivers of change. It's more a matter of them filling a void that was often seen as mysterious or even linked to religious beliefs – "It was God's doing." The real challenge for businesses, however, is to come up with something; to invent something that solves a customer problem or makes customers' lives a bit easier. And this is the real "wild knowledge" that companies are looking for. Finding and taming "wild knowledge" and the technology linked to it, before someone else does, helps us to hold on to the lead position by re-inventing our company and ourselves, over and over again We can create temporary monopolies, and that is the real driver in any market economy.

Today, one of the biggest problems for ideas and creativity is that we want to measure everything. We want to be in control. As soon as we have the opportunity we want to plug it into models and methodologies and reports so that we can measure its progress. The process of finding ideas involves considering all possibilities, visualizing and looking ahead. During this process, we tend to start analyzing and evaluating from the outset, while the ideal sequence would call for retrospective analysis and evaluation once this journey has ended. These should always be subsequent steps and not parallel activities.

Fear of not having control (or the fear of ambiguity) is another common methodology error. We want to explain why things happen and to have things add up. But this is not how the world works, as there will always be things that you do not understand and great ideas often emerge from chaos. Management thinker and author

Marcus Buckingham wrote one of his bestselling books, *First, Break All The Rules*, on this very topic. We do not always know why, but some things work better than anything we may have done before. Afterwards our analytical mind can try to come up with some self-styled plausibility to justify this. Regardless of how you do it, you need to find ways to accept the messy parts, or parts that do not follow any model or structure. Remember, it is not a weakness to accept things that work out nicely even when you do not understand why. Just let go… and go with it.

Putting everything into models and structures might also lead to what is referred to as "analysis paralysis". This is when you are so focused on gathering as much information as possible – or when you spend so much time thinking about a problem – that your mind brims over and you lose the ability to act. Success lies in the ability to stop collecting information at the right time so that you can proceed with real, results-oriented action.

Whatever it is you chose, you need to step out of your comfort zone. What will be taken for granted tomorrow is something that might seem impossible today. Do not limit yourself to past experiences. Instead, seek new ones.

"All truth passes through three stages. First, it is ridiculed. Second, it is violently opposed. Third, it is accepted as being self-evident."

– Arthur Schopenhauer

A technique that is often undervalued is what we call "availability bias" or "availability heuristic". This is essentially a mental shortcut for decision makers that gives preference to more recent information and events. With this method of thinking, we relate to our personal experience with a given topic, concept, method or decision. Since we can easily recall it or comfortably relate to it, we believe it is valid and important, or at least see it as more important than the alternatives. Based on the biases of previous experience, or recalled information and emotions, we judge future topics.

Adding to this is the maturing – and our own understanding – of the internet and social media. Digital media have undoubtedly sped up how we connect and unite throughout the world. But what was once thought to be the universal remedy for liberating societies and connecting us has more recently revealed its shortcomings.

We now face the challenge of dealing with rumors that spread across these channels, to millions of people, in an extraordinarily short period of time. We have self-created echo chambers where we co-create truth within the biases of the group of people we follow and believe in. We unfollow, mute or block any other opinions, and it is difficult to change opinions once they gain momentum. We are forced to jump to conclusions on opinions packed into 140 characters, when what is at issue are complex global topics that trigger emotions and spark harsh debate. We forget that behind online avatars there are actual human beings. And once published and pushed, we are not interested in changing our views, even if it later turns out there is new, contradictory evidence. Today's channels of communication can be as powerful and provocative as the radio was in the days of Adolf Hitler. We see it with Donald Trump, ISIS, and the right-wing movements in Europe. With this polarization, technology then becomes the problem and not the solution.

Thinking is difficult, and takes time, so we often prefer to judge based on how ideas and thoughts are presented and what we have seen on social media. We do not have time to work through the questions, so we go with our judgment. Overwhelmed by a flood of information and distracted by things that eat up our time and attention, the masses accept a presumed answer based on disturbed judgments. Our answers and reasoning are not even plausible to ourselves, if we really think about it, but we move on nonetheless.

To offset today's preponderance of one-sided, sensational, angry posts we need to work on these structures and enable channels that deliver some sort of affirmation and reward for being thoughtful and civil. Instead of rewarding the sheer numerical weight of clicks and page views, we need to find ways to foster higher-quality conversation. Instead of measuring total number of readers, we should spotlight posts when influential people – those with societal impact – read and respond to them. Additionally, we need to make it socially acceptable to change opinions, reward constructive disagreement and encourage open dialogue, instead of simply broadcasting rote opinions.

We can work for this sort of change by spending time with people of a different mindset than our own – those from different backgrounds, who possess a rich diversity of experiences. There is value in looking at others as inspiration for overcoming our own limitations. As far as social media is concerned, we do not yet have all the answers. But we need to be open to thoughtful discussions, and we need to tame the technology and liberate the internet with new methods and methodologies… all in the service of the creation and distribution of ideas.

THE SUCCESS FORMULA – COLLABORATION

A model that has worked since we started hunting lions on the savannahs and building pyramids near the sandy stretches of the Nile is collaboration. Today, as complexity increases, collaboration is even more crucial. There is much to be gained by diverse groups working across assumed differences. Younger generations will be in a better place if we also work to equip them for change. Too many are frustrated because we do not tolerate or understand their opinions. Success lies in promoting co-creation and conversation. Not just any conversation, but a deeper dialogue on radical opinions, a place where even the worst of enemies can comfortably come together, respect each other and create new solutions.

Our progress as a society hinges on creating a collective "WE". It's all about interdependency and the exploration of similarities, as opposed to the friction of differences that drives the field of IDEAS. Within the groups we define – whether by race, gender, interests or financial class – we are moving together as we go to the borders of our differences to exploit ideas. However you choose to put it, collaboration is essential. The assumption here is that the greater our differences, the richer our collective palette of viewpoints will be.

If we take a look behind the scenes, co-creating – or collaborating – has very much been the formula for success throughout history. One example, as we return to the great Thomas Edison, is the team approach, a culture of participation and creation hub. Edison would gather collaborators for his so-called "Midnight Lunch" (a concept described in Sarah Miller Caldicott's book of the same title). Edison used to return to his laboratory in the evenings to discuss ideas with his team of 8-9 people. As they tried out various ideas – adapting, copying from other fields and exchanging their thoughts – they were transformed from a group of employees into a true team of colleagues. And from there on out, they continued to learn important lessons about collaborative idea development, co-creating new thoughts.

But be careful. This kind of collaboration is not what you get when today's large corporations take a few dozen 50-year-old white men from middle/senior management, dressed in dark suits, all from the same few universities, fold then into a controlling department with rigid KPIs and ROIs, and task then with formulating innovative new ideas. How the hell do you expect something to come out of that? Ideally, the teams should be small – 2-8 people in a group that includes both experts and generalists, with mutual TRUST and a common objective. These individuals need to feel a sense of openness, and the conviction that failing is not an option. Creating is LEARNING, not only executing tasks. The collaborative approach to new learning is to question the answers "given". In many cases (or should I say in most... no, in ALL cases) there needs to be a balance. Certain overriding dynamics must be respected. The skills and imaginative thinking of so-called creative people – whether they are right-brained or left-brained need to be paired with input from those who are stronger at structure and execution. However, in the creative process, the force and the law of thinking must be respected. Very few organizations think about it in this way when working on change and trying to form a "special taskforce" for coming up with new ideas.

No ideas are good in the beginning. I have been in many meetings, particularly in larger corporations, where ideas, or the creative people who generate them, are thwarted by "naysayers". I have seen these obstructionists demolish the creation process by uttering a simple "yes, but..." It is time for these people to step aside and let the fruitcakes and the crazies run the party. There is so much to be gained as we explore the possibilities of co-creating and collaboration across mindsets, experiences, and diverse backgrounds and opinions. An advertisement for this approach could honestly state, "Money-Back Guarantee". Try it; you can always revert back to the old order if you are not happy with the results.

DREAMS
& FLOWS

*"Bye-Bye Bullshit!
Now is the time
to stop tolerating."*

I would like to round off this section by looking at the human component in the concept of "IDEAS". Let us again look at the concept of "mensch". We'll also look at the ebb and flow of knowledge in recent times and take a closer look at how we move up and down the ladder of consciousness.

In our unconscious state of mind, we dream. The beauty of dreaming is that it allows us to drift off to new realities and wander up and down the ladder of creation and imagination. The way we think about progress, and many of our achievements, have evolved out of dreams – through the simple act of igniting small ideas.

But let's start with something simpler. Imagine the newspaper headline about your company 20 years from now, or a headline about you personally. What would it say? You should write your ideal headline on the wall. Put it down as a goal – a dream, if you will – and then go after it. Your dreams about a potential personal future can be really strong. If you write them down, they will happen. If you see it in your dreams, it will happen. There are so many examples of how people have dreamed up a pre-defined future. This has been the case throughout history, although in today's hectic world too many people are oblivious to the possibilities. And that makes it difficult for them to visualize and dream. So many quit because they think the road is too long, or that they will fail. But if you have this dream that envisions the future, it becomes more than just a picture on the lower scale of the consciousness; it will become increasingly clear as you follow your (vivid) image. A dream might offer the guidance that will eventually lead you somewhere. The difference is if you can see it. And, as stated in the beginning, we now have the power to do whatever we want – we are all "do-doers", yet we need something that we can envision. What is your vision of the world? What do you dream of? What would make you happy?

Act out your dream with open eyes – ignore the tumult of the real world. Dare to speak it out loud. Too many people keep their thoughts to themselves. If you practice being with your thoughts and emphasize your inner story, you will eventually be able to reach what we call a flow state.

A state of flow is where you envision something. It is a clear-eyed state, where everything is in focus, and together, your dream and your combined experience, wisdom and knowledge become extremely powerful.

There are many examples of geniuses of the past who entered into a state of flow while realizing their ideas, performing their art, achieving their full creative potential. And though it may seem like a dream, and you feel light and clear when you are "in the flow", we have to realize that there is no stairway to heaven, no linear or exponential line that goes directly *up there*. Even in the state of flow, there is no evidence that you will realize immediate success or celebrate ongoing success. To get to this state you often have to withstand some very challenging resistance. One artist who was definitely in a flow of creation was Vincent van Gogh. He produced more than 2,000 paintings but sold only one during his lifetime – *La Vigne Rouge* (the Red Vineyard) – before committing suicide at age 37. While van Gogh did not succeed during his time on Earth, there are examples of others who mastered the pressure and truly took it to the next stage. One is "human brand" Michael Jordan, who was kicked off his high school basketball team because he was not good enough... only to return as one of the greatest players in history. Oprah Winfrey was told she was not suited for television. Walt Disney was told he had no imagination. These are all examples of people from humble origins, with big dreams, rewriting history in diverse fields of flow.

Finding the flow – or being in a flow state – is something we track back to Chinese philosophy. Around 500 BC the founders of the philosophical term Taoism, and the thinkers Confucious and Laozi (also called Lao-Tzu or Lao-Tze, which literally means "the old master"), worked on accessing Wu Wei, a state of spontaneous flow, which literally means *non-action* or *non-doing*. The ancient Chinese would use meditation and rituals to reach this state; it was something that people were willing to go extraordinary lengths to achieve. In sports this is often referred to as a state of consciousness that puts you "in the moment", or being "in the zone". Time seems to slow down, you block out all surrounding sounds, and you are capable of focusing intensively, with all your passion, on what you are doing. Artists also cite this as a state where they lose track of time and perform at a level they'd only dreamed of.

You do not enter the zone whenever you like or when you simply think about it. Instead, when you are playing the game fully, with love and passion, one can say the zone finds you or rewards you for your practice, focus and dedication. It is the state that Vincent van Gogh and so many artists reached, where abstraction, and the simplified form of the totality and genius of dreams flow and are projected onto the physical world. As was the case with Van Gogh, it is not always recognized at the time and many quit before understanding their own mastery, achievements, or potential for achievement.

But this state of "being in the zone" is not luck or something someone simply has, but the result of the workouts where you stayed at it – even after you were tired and sore – and put in the extra effort. Our greatest limitations come from experience and history. We have to let go and live according to our imagination.

Flow can come out of a trusted environment, out of collegiality. You need to be in and around a team where you feel you can step up and get work done. On the court at a sports event, people look anxiously to one another when it comes to taking the final shot, as if there is a strong feeling of confidence and belief that magic will happen. For artists, the state of flow is not something that just strikes out of nowhere, but something that very often evolves out of the process. Authors often say something like, "I keep staring at a blank piece of paper until blood drips from my forehead... and then I begin typing."

But what if our world is in fact only an outcome of what we believe we can achieve, coming solely from our dreams? Maybe dreams are that powerful. But what limits our imagination? Will we come closer to solving the mysteries of dreams and the state of flow?

Dreams, being in a state of flow, starting over (and over and over again) and serendipity – taken together, that's what brings ideas to life.

All companies are looking for this; we are intoxicated by start-up dreams and the promise of innovation, both vertical and horizontal. And it is a beautiful thing that everyone can be a part of. Starting, shaping, trying, failing, learning, copying and stealing, getting lucky, changing existing models and working with diverse, interesting people. At the end of the day, there is no stronger you than you. You can make an impact every day with your *failtastic* way of being "mensch".

Leaders of larger corporations or successful business people come to me and ask, "What should I do?" My answer is simple: "Go away and dream it up all over again."

CHAPTER III
FOCUS &
SIMPLICITY

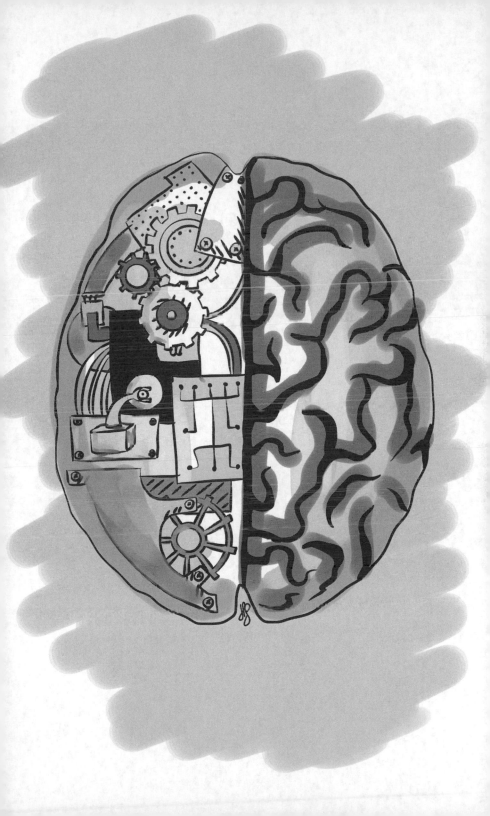

"The aspects of things that are most important to us are hidden because of their simplicity and familiarity."

– Ludwig Wittgenstein

One day, at lunch with one of my creative colleagues, I was asked the question of all questions. "Anders," he asked, "in what language do you think?" I looked at him and trotted out my regular answer: "An odd question, and one that I keep getting asked," I said. And then I turned it around, as I always do, and asked right back, "In what language do YOU think?"

As a German guy through-and-through, he gave me a confused look, obviously wondering why I would even ask that. His response was clear and conventionally structured: "German!" But, with my background in multilingualism, I had been asked this question on many occasions over the years, and it had grown somewhat irritating.

"You see, I don't know," I continued. "I simply don't think in any particular language, or in spoken words. Yes, there are conversations I conduct in my head, and in those instances, I have noticed that I tend to do it in the language most relevant to the topic, or the language I want to express myself in. But I think, in my inner-most thoughts, in visual images. The self-conversation is just a very small part of how we think."

I guess he was somewhat convinced by my answer, but also confused. Although, as a philosopher and a student of the art of thinking, I had given this answer many times before, this time I was prompted to turn to science and take a closer look at this question.

I found that there was a lot of literature on the topic. And so, I could finally relax in the knowledge that I was not some weirdo simply because I did not think like everyone else. If you were to ask yourself the same question and really think about it, the words that we speak or write are an oral or visual form of expression, an analog of what our mind is producing. But there is so much more to it, more than just the core of thought related to one particular language. The language of thought is independent of the language we're speaking and is instead a more fundamental, universal form of human communication.

But spoken language – the articulation of a limited pool of words to express our thoughts – is only a very small part of the process. First we visualize the monologue, then we paint the picture. We create mental models and visual maps that are our definition of the "real world". They are mapped using our experiences and previously stored knowledge. That old saying, "Think before you speak," means nothing more than "prepare". This is certainly important in many cases, but it dampens creativity and spontaneity.

One philosophical concept that I have developed over time is what I call "thinking out loud". When the Pope asked Michelangelo how he created his masterpiece, the famous statue of David, the artist replied, "I just removed everything that was not David." In what language did he do that?

If you were to think about the feeling of a sharp knife, or the taste of that strawberry picked fresh from the garden, or the cloud of smoke you pass through when walking past someone with a cigarette – what is the language of these thoughts? All of these perceptions are built on our experiences, our habits and senses, our mental models – how we have captured and defined the stuff in our minds – and our own unique grasp of the "real world". The slamming of a door. The crying of a baby. What is the language of these thoughts?

Cognitive science and linguistics teach us that we need to distinguish between our internal visualization of words – our own monologues – and the actual thoughts behind them. In this case, think about what is the language of your goal, what is the language of sound, of smell, of pictures, of images and of objects. What about the name or the thing that you cannot remember, that sits on the tip of your tongue? What language is this thought?

The art of thinking takes us all the way back to Plato's famous Allegory of the Cave, which explored how we perceive reality. And regardless of the angle from which we look at it, we know that thought goes much deeper than merely the question, "In what language do you think?" The art of thinking goes beyond our consciousness and is related to a subjective view of our self-proclaimed reality.

In many ways, I believe we are still in Plato's cave and that by sorting the "wild knowledge" we will move on. This beautiful capacity for thought, creativity and the art of thinking is, I'd suggest, the journey of the "Mensch". Technology is replacing our defined left brain activities, including thinking in words and language. We don't know what thinking is, or how or where it exists. We can think about everything, reflect, and think about that. We can think about the thinking itself! Many things are still unknown to us. We turn to God and religion for the answers, or rely on the progress of science.

Notions of reincarnation and infinity rooted in ancient Indian and Egyptian belief systems, which Neitzsche picked up on, can provide an easy way out. But perhaps more than anything, it is our unlimited capacity for thinking that defines us as human. As the French philosopher Blaise Pascal put it, "L'homme est un Roseau pensant" – *Man is a thinking reed*. He saw man as "a weak being/object who, however, controls nature through the help of thinking."

The challenge is not what to think, but how to think. Learning how to think is simply continuous learning. In a time when we are moving rapidly from IQ to EQ (the so-called Emotional Quotient), we are, as I've said, potentially the last IQ-Generation. The logical and analytical part of our brains may be replaced by machines but thinking will set us apart, a point I believe to be crucial. I believe that we will be in bad shape as soon as we start tapping our brains onto "the net" – the collective knowledge machine. I believe that we should create AI, the machines, and the future, but we should not attach our mysterious consciousness – our capacity to forget, unlearn and make mistakes – to a machine that will eradicate these vital attributes. But we are talking about simplification, right? Making everything easier and actually *thinking* is hard work, isn't it?

The infinite part of thinking is an incomplete infinity; it is an infusible contradiction. We do not know how far knowledge and thought can reach in relation to the totality of our reality. Thinking is uncontrolled, and the knowledge created is wild. In unconsciousness, when we sleep, we create thoughts. Only a small portion of this can be controlled; it shows up in our lost and deep thoughts. We have created linguistic terms such as "day-dreaming," "on the tip of my tongue," and "out of my mind," but thoughts evolved at a deeper level than our ability to describe them in words.

Thoughts are thought, they might not be written or spoken, and in hindsight we remember these moments with, "I should have written that down." Or all those "in the shower moments" – the fleeting, seemingly random recollection of thoughts and ideas that got lost.

As we discussed in the "IDEAS" section, these thoughts (or ideas) – whether horizontal or vertical – are important, as they help in our adaptation to the existing world and drive innovation. But a second look teaches us that these "innovations" really change the world.

The most effective way of becoming a better thinker, and finding your own thoughts, is simply to probe other people's thoughts. It is not about having the right answers, but about asking the right questions. The simplest of all questions is, "Why?" This opens the doors to your own thoughts in so many ways. There is also "cause-and-effect" problem solving, utilizing the 5W methodology – simply asking *why*, five times, to get to the bottom of a problem. The "5" comes out of an empirical study on the number of iterations typically required to resolve a given problem. The technique was originally developed by Sakichi Toyoda, and was at the heart of his Toyota Motor Corp. when the Japanese automaker devised its revolutionary manufacturing methodologies. The 5W approach has since been applied by many other companies – with varying numbers of the question "Why?" – to broaden goal-setting and decision-making processes.

The future will, as always, be really boring, predictable and simple, as if we all saw it coming. As we have done in the past, we will take technological breakthroughs for granted. Best-selling author and researcher Tom Rath reinforces this point by saying, "What you will be most proud of a decade from now will not be anything that was a result of you simply responding." Instead, he suggests, "Manage communications, online and offline, instead of letting the communication run your life simply by acting upon something in reactive mode. This is dangerous, as you end up spending a majority of your time just responding to other people's needs instead of creating anything that lasts." Whatever technological or scientific progress give us, the leaders of the future will again be those turning inward and using the full power of their own minds to challenge this. They will do so by what I call "thinking out loud".

Today, most of us spend too little time thinking and reflecting about what we really want. There should be a dedicated "thinking hour" that managers and leaders regularly schedule into their calendars. But, due to our ravenous consumption of media and data today, progress can only come out of dialogue and interaction with people offering different values, thoughts and backgrounds. Therefore, the concept of "thinking out loud" is not only a road to sorting out one's unstructured wild knowledge – and mapping it, through simplification, to old or new mental models – but also a collaborative form of interaction to jointly create new thoughts and mindsets. We see this in particular with the younger generation. Whereas with previous generations the goal was to hide and protect knowledge at any cost – out of fear of losing exclusivity and forfeiting control – today the only preferred option is to share and co-create. Gone are the wisdom dinosaurs. Today's young people are more like Lego blocks – they want to be a part of the bigger, interlinked whole. We call this participatory culture.

Personally, I have had many experiences with "thinking out loud", where the discussions, creativity and flow led to self-awareness and defined a clearer picture of what I wanted to achieve. Listening to the outcome of a discussion helps me sort my thoughts and then, later, to go back and clarify through deeper reflection and thinking. This is a good exercise for figuring out what you really mean. Talking about things that are disturbing, or things that are not appropriate or "right," can also be a good practice. When we say, "That's a problem," it doesn't necessarily mean it is bad. It just means that it could be even better, and speaking about it will help you move in the right direction. There is seldom only one road, or just one solution, so you have to choose a path. By "thinking out loud" you have support in doing this.

Many of us see the headlines in today's media and form our opinions accordingly. Whether we call it "critical thinking" or "creative thinking" the focus should be on neither critical nor creative considerations. Rather, we should be focusing on the "thinking" part.

A big problem with our views is that they are swayed by the media, influencers, colleagues and the environment. But we should do more to get inspired by great thinkers and see that there is room for new discoveries. Today we think most things are so easy or obvious that anyone can nail them, and the rest we see as impossible. But we should continue to look for secrets, through science and technology. Looking at companies such as Uber and Airbnb, we see that the simplest of business needs and models can lead to great success, because that's what customers want, sometimes without even knowing that they want it. Only by challenging our thoughts will more of these innovative business models arise and flourish. Thinking critically and asking questions go hand-in-hand. What secrets is nature not telling you? What secrets are people not telling you?

The importance of what I call "thinking out loud" resonates all the way back to the first true (and maybe the greatest) philosopher, Plato, who 2,400 years ago devoted his life to helping people reach "Eudaimonia" – fulfillment. He wrote 36 books during his life based on four big, core ideas. According to Plato, we need to think more, as we rarely give ourselves time to think carefully and logically about our life and how to lead it. This is even truer today than it was 2,400 years ago. We tend to go along with what the Greeks called "DOXA", or what we know as popular opinion. Plato states the importance of knowing yourself and working through a special kind of therapy: philosophy. You should explore and examine rather than just act on impulses. Voting for Donald Trump, the rise of far-right movements, and frustration with the European Union are typical examples of this. If you go out and strengthen your knowledge, then you will not get distracted or be led by your feelings. On this note, Plato's mentor and friend, Socrates, gave name to what we today call the Socratic Discussion. This is basically thinking out loud, where you sort through your thoughts and ideas by talking to a friend who wants to help you become clearer.

NARROW IT! RIGHT THINGS RIGHT (FIRST)

"*Effective leadership is putting first things first. Effective management is discipline, carrying it out.*"

– Stephen R. Covey

This will not be a short chapter. However, I will narrow it down and start with the most important (right) things and get them right (first), before exploring some core concepts and thoughts on how to achieve the right focus. In a world filled with opportunities and a business environment of increasing complexity, we need to learn how to close some doors, to shut out irrelevant options. Too much information leads to false influences on how we act. It may even influence something I call a *Bauchgefühlkurzschluss*, or a "Gut-Feeling-Short-Circuit".

A Gut-Feeling-Short-Circuit is basically something that occurs when we cannot relate to our experiences, our wisdom – what we call "Gut-Feeling". Change occurs through a physiological connection between brain and heart. It is when we make decisions under the influence of an external factor that distracts our decision-making. When there are multiple priorities (an oxymoron), our energy is expended disproportionately and things become bogged down. So narrowing and doing the right things right (first) means being clear and very specific. How much can you tighten up your explanation of who and what you would really like to be, or what you hope to achieve? Can you put it into 2-3 words? One sentence? Can you be the king of the one-liners and simply get things done?

Operational excellence, execution, getting things done – that is what we are all told to do, but problems arise when you get conflicting impulses, and other, distracting thoughts and ideas enter your mind. What should you do? Doing the right things right (first) does not mean you should not apply your thoughts and ideas and seek new opportunities in a world of change. What it does mean is that on some occasions you should take a more structured, or a more rational, approach. Simplification calls for eliminating anything that is irrelevant in order to have the relevant stuff shine through. Knowing what's most important to you or your organization puts everything else into context. If it doesn't serve your top priority, then it's a distraction. Period.

In a world of chaos, we need more chaos for new solutions, but we also need structure. If you feel chaos in your organization, first understand that all progress is at times chaotic... and go with it, respect it. From an operational standpoint, though, you need to narrow the focus and apply the right things correctly, first by assigning singular responsibilities. From a management standpoint, making every person in the company responsible for doing just one thing will make people unique. It is not only about value and providing a sense of purpose, but also about transparency and simplification. It's about working through how to identify, evaluate and replicate operational excellence. Simplifying the task of managing people and defining roles reduces conflict and streamlines a lot of the wild knowledge floating around out there. Political battlefields emerge as people fight over the same ownership and responsibility.

It is crucial for us to recognize that there is no "one-size-fits-all" in the business world. At some point you have to execute and get things done, while at the same time exploiting wild knowledge and finding ideas. As much as I am a driver of change, of ideas and creation, and have a passion for driving change through the art of thinking, I also have respect for the importance of getting things done. There is value in getting things sorted in order to do right things right (first), and that begins with simply gathering them. With emerging new tools and technologies this has become a very efficient way of working. The simplest form of this is to create a folder in your inbox that replaces your physical notebook – a place where you can send yourself e-mails for reference – or by using a "thoughts & ideas" app as your tool. Maybe this is the modern way of structuring what French poet and novelist Victor Hugo had in mind when he famously said, "Nothing is more powerful than an idea whose time has come." In order to keep the right focus and get things done, you can, and should, save your ideas and thoughts in a way that makes them readily available to you. Make sure you return to them every week, or at least once a month, as these things can become unimportant over time. Then plan your time accordingly, so you can put your thoughts into action, and keep a relatively clean desk, without losing focus.

I have learned that keeping things simple is in fact really complex. It can also be quite frustrating. In particular, this is the case with business start-ups. Many young entrepreneurs whom I have worked with spend endless nights discussing innovative ideas: "What can we add?" or "What kinds of features should be included?" In most situations I challenge this with the questions, "What can we take out?" or "How can we streamline it?" History shows us that launching a product in its simplest state will help to identify what customers really want, and reveal how they will use a product or service. In order to do this effectively, you need to simplify and just "let go". You need to give up some control to the people who are going to use what you're building, and effectively reduce your own "powers". You need to let go of things that are not crucial to your product or service. One example of this is Larry Wall, who created a programming language called Perl. Wall was quoted as saying, "When they built the University of California at Irvine they just put the buildings in. They did not put in any sidewalks; they just planted grass. The next year, they came back and put the sidewalks where the trails were in the grass." His point here was that Perl was not designed on first principles; it was instead analogous to those sidewalks. This should be on your mind when you create your app, or your tool, or work on your concepts. Customer usage patterns will help to simplify your product and make it better.

Progress also comes from breaking down goals and tasks to "micro-resolutions". Basically, this is about thinking small before seeing the big picture. The execution of small steps eventually leads you to the big breakthrough idea or achievement. It leads you toward what you or your environment define as success. By sharpening the focus on the small steps you will be able to zero-in on the objective that leads to success. You will fail to reach the bigger goals if you continuously follow, track and measure these. They will sap your power and motivation, and prevent you from feeling the progress that is needed to continue. In her book, *Small Move, Big Change*, Caroline Arnold, who built the auction system for Google's IPO and is a Wall Street innovator, discusses using micro-resolutions to transform. Arnold uses her own life as a case study, contrasting her career successes with her resolution failures. She even includes tasks that can take a lot of energy, like going to the gym or the internal-external pressures of trying to spend more time with her family. After experiencing a painful failure, Arnold decided to focus on small but meaningful behavioral changes. By executing and narrowing her own focus, she "accidentally" discovered a method for transformation, one where clear commitments were reached almost every time, building the foundation for continuous progress.

Living in this age of big data, we tend to mix up the concept of order and disorder. Disorder, or chaos, is not the opposite of order. Having more data and information does not lead to a better result, a better fit or greater order. No, it is about adding more chaos and creation, while narrowing your focus and "getting things done", and by applying the "right things right" principle. Digitizing a bad process will not make it good; it is not about technology for technology's sake, but more the focus of getting the right things lined up and sorted out. We do not have the questions, yet we have wisdom and knowledge saved, so the challenge is for our consciousness to tap into this knowledge when it is needed. Even more important than applying big data, and known, structured knowledge, today it is crucial to find the right degree of simplification. In science, achieving ever-simpler theories is a driving force. Instead of big data, it is all about the right data.

Over the years, a problem I have seen in many organizations is the narrowed focus on success, or self-described success. We look at and celebrate the geniuses of our paradigm without understanding the process. But, as almost all innovators and creators of modern times state over and over again, there are so many things that we can learn from the many failures of the past. Yet these concepts are not applied in management and leadership thinking. There are many reasons why mature companies, start-ups and organizations of all sorts fail. Incremental failure is a part of any organization, and we should not be so afraid of it. In fact, most organizations need to learn how to be open to failure and create a culture that is comfortable with it. There are so many things to learn from failure, lessons that will keep us moving forward. Often, though, we get too busy copying any success or achievement that comes along, even when they are the result of plain old luck. With all due respect, it is extremely difficult to replicate luck. Instead of replicating success formulas and trying to copy patterns of luck, we must refine our mode of execution by learning from our previous failures. Only then will we be able to see new opportunities hidden in plain sight.

When we set out to narrow our focus and do the right things right (first), we must understand that human capital is still the core asset… and misusing it by over-demanding attention destroys any form of simplicity. When I look at entrepreneurs and start-ups, this is a crucial topic for evaluation. Are the founders 100% committed and focused on their idea, their concept, and their business? Or are they tempted to be sucked into the paradox of various opportunities, which will not only lead to disaster for the investor but eventually to frustration and failure for the owners. The point here is not to offer an investor's guide or a "to-do" list for entrepreneurs, but to examine a paradox found within many organizations today. Yet we should keep a broad view and not get button-holed into an expert's mindset. There is so much to learn by narrowing focus in terms of how we lead organizations and drive change. The key is that the wrong focus will send you drifting off track faster than you will be able to recover.

Although we have created all kinds of management tools and technologies to support us, our consciousness and the state of being *fully conscious* seem to be a limitation for us. But with these challenges, I believe we should both embrace a broad view and carry a narrowed-view skillset in order to get things done.

A core strength, I believe, is to throw out the additional weight and baggage and simplify, to get a clear overview of what is really important. For me, this applies at the collective level as well as the individual level. It is a mindset – a set of guideposts that can be useful when navigating one's own structures.

The philosopher Diogenes, who pursued the simplest form of living, once saw a poor peasant boy drink water from the hollow of his hands. Seeing this, Diogenes destroyed his single worldly possession – a simple wooden bowl. "Fool that I am," he said, "to have been carrying superfluous baggage all this time!" Likewise, elements of the technology available to us today make our lives easier and support us in our work, but not in every way.

Business today, and our lives in general, still have much room for improvements. There is room to take back the control of our choices and to strive for meaning and happiness, but not at the costs of complexity and extra weight. For businesses, owning everything was once thought to be a "best practice". This is not only proved to be costly, but it makes one carry more "weight", which eventually slows you down. Instead of fighting for the best price, the question should be: what can we borrow or lease that we are currently buying outright, or planning to buy? There are even free services and other options on the market today for organizations and start-ups to embrace.

Getting things right is not only about tasks, process, technology and losing focus. When it comes to the early stages of businesses, I have identified a crucial pattern that explains why businesses do not succeed at first. Very often it is related to the partners involved. Having the right partners is crucial. A business partnership is like a marriage; this I have experienced myself for good and for bad. I have seen people change, witnessed the influence of money, and observed how egos get in the way. And when things boil down to a clash of monumental egos, there can be only one winner: the lawyer.

A final topic that we will take a look at in this chapter on finding the right focus is the phenomenon of "decision fatigue". In psychology and in the study of decision making, decision fatigue refers to the reduced quality of decisions made when there are too many to be made and too much work required to make them. From modern leadership biographies we learn that one of the tried-and-true criteria for success is to make fewer decisions in order to make better decisions. Steve Jobs and Mark Zuckerberg provide compelling examples of how focus improves decision-making. They simplified their days, for example, by avoiding a monotonous, time-consuming task: deciding what to wear in the morning. Instead, they wore the same clothes every day. When we look at artists, they may seem to live boring lives because they focus all of their time and energy on their art. They narrow their thoughts and decisions to their prime function, to the exclusion of virtually everything else. Essentially, they do the right things right (first) by simplifying the total sum of their senses and experiences to intensive moments of creation. What we can learn from this is that you need to drop the decisions that you do not have to make. This will give you more energy and focus for the truly important decisions.

In the 21st Century, people are far too driven by external factors,; they are heavily influenced by these forces of change. We feel the pressure to "always be on" and to make decisions on any given topic at any time. It is not that we should dedicate ourselves to living boring lives, or having tunnel-vision on one topic, but we need to become consciously aware of the energy we waste by having to make unnecessary decisions. In fact, you may learn that there is nothing wrong with being a bit boring at times. Nothing of importance goes away if you just "log off" for a short period of time. You can be present in any particular moment, but the secret is to shut down the engine every now and then, even if it means just wearing the same t-shirt to work every day. (Some stores offer 3-for-1 clothing deals, which can be helpful from a personal hygiene standpoint.) This streamlining of decision-making also encourages us to get a lot more work done. Periods where people are boring can be when the most work gets done, thanks to focused progress. This is where you can benefit from some essential business learning (aka "takeaways").

Life is really simple, but we insist on making it complicated.
– Confucius

THE
EQUATION

Let's do maths! I love maths! By the end of the sixth grade I had mastered ninth grade maths books, and given my enthusiasm for sports after-hours, it was not through additional work at home but rather passion and effort brought to bear during school hours. This passion was also how I began my journey into the world of creativity and ideas and found my interest in philosophy, consciousness, and exploration of the mind, all of which may seem odd to many. Let's just say that life and learning are not always linear. Looking back, I cannot see clear developmental patterns, but the equation still adds up for me. It is kind of like "a x b x c – d", where "d" can be replaced by "e, f, g, h" – you get it. We put too much effort into trying to define the logic of what we have done. Unless our every move in life is consciously plotted out – with a driving passion, a well-defined goal and a strategically charted path – we should just accept that life is not predictable. There is no algorithm or equation that adds up to X (with X being our life), where we can look back and say, "Man, that turned out just as I'd predicted." In the final analysis, we should be pleased if we can say, "It all turned out pretty well." In the end, this is all about values, not about the equations.

I am not stating that mathematics is not important, but even maths has been disrupted in the 21st Century. Applying maths to the physical world is something we do every day. We read headlines, add it all up and draw conclusions. Knowledge, we call it... but we are wrong. Our inner equation adds up to "the world is terrible." But in fact, when we look at the numbers, it has never been more peaceful. Today, if a person dies in Bavaria, the whole world knows. Yet, just 20 years ago, if a village of 3,000 people was slaughtered in Afghanistan, no one outside the immediate vicinity would have known. Pervasive access to information brings not only the facts into our homes but also a sense of empathy. We feel closer and more connected, and increasingly find ourselves tapping into the "feel" of what is going on in the world around us. In our current paradigm and based on where we are today, we can have difficulty coping with this state. Instead of understanding the impacts of an interdependently connected world, and the challenges aligned with the opportunities and upsides of globalization, we freak out. This should serve as a valuable lesson.

Finding the right focus and simplifying our lives, amidst the complex information fed to us by the media, overwhelms us and puts our minds in a state of frustration. Only at the peak of human excellence can we achieve a state of focus where we can effectively use analytics to discover and invent new truths.

Amassing numbers and data, and using historical formulas or patterns to justify knowledge, is often how we operate. With its mountains of data and analysis-driven approach, Google set out to research what makes a productive, "perfect" team. The internet giant spent years gathering information and feeding it through various analyses. This undertaking, which the company called "Project Aristotle", concluded that the search for a magic formula was the wrong approach entirely. Instead, what Google found was something we have been reading about for years in successive waves of management books. It featured prominently in *The 7 Habits of Highly Effective People*, by the late Dr. Stephen R. Covey. When I met Dr. Covey back in 2010, he summed up what would also be the conclusion of Google's analysis: "Seek first to understand, then to be understood." So, a successful team is one where the members respect each other's emotions. No hidden formula, no new math.

There are many examples of how vicious wisdom runs contrary to our presumed knowledge, becoming what we call "unconventional wisdom" when applied to our daily lives. By visualizing and breaking data down into a simplified form, Prof. Hans Roßling, a Swedish statistician, has inspired the world with his reframing of globalization, as he did with his TED Talk on "global populations". Referred to by the *Telegraph* as the "man who makes statistics sing," Through his GAPminder Foundation, Prof. Roßling gives us a clarified statistical view of the world based on actual data, instead of through the prism of news headlines. He carried out what he called an "ignorance study" to show that regardless of how high we climb the academic ladder; human beings still know as little about the world as chimpanzees. His study examined big-picture global issues: climate change, health, poverty and population. He demonstrated that what we think we know, in our ignorance and arrogance – what we call mankind's knowledge – is merely an illusion that is forced on us by the day's headlines. Prof. Roßling and the GAPMinder team show us the true problem with media and how, in today's society we burrow ourselves into a state of ignorance and subsequently develop deep-seated frustrations.

We simplify and try to connect to models, but as we only see one side of the coin, we do not take an actual knowledge-based approach to achieving wisdom. We rush to apply this presumed knowledge to our daily lives based on false assumptions. The impact? Chaos across industries, borders, political parties, belief systems, and across interest groups and defined "communities" or "cultures". Is this bad? Or is it good? Now what?

Algorithms and software are eating the world. The relentless flood of information is having an undeniable impact on our lives. Computers are making our decisions, and their ascendancy in logical, left-brain activities is something that HAS ALREADY HAPPENED. I suggested earlier that we may be seeing the last IQ-Generation. We simply do not know where it all will lead. Whatever the numbers may be, information and IQ are still only small pieces of our human totality. Let's do some simple analysis and maths.

If I laid down six matchsticks so they spelled out this simple equation – XI + I = X – how many matches do you need to move to get this equation to logically add up? This is a question I regularly ask my audience, and I always see the super-confident guy answering as if it was a complex puzzle to solve. We are not only wired by our analytical thinking but also by our own ego. This was best illustrated for me in November 2015 when I sat down with a school class outside of Mumbai, India. I asked the teacher for a session with the kids... only I would be the student and they would be the teachers. We talked about the challenges of the modern world and the problems we face, and a 12-year-old summed it up with this observation: "Uncle, the biggest problem in the world today is our ego."

The answer to my maths question above? "You just need to move one match." I will hear this across the room, from the confident guy, who is almost always seated in one of the first three rows. "One move, very good – that is a low number," I answer. "You must have studied." I even let him explain how you can move the one match from the left side to the right side, making it a matchstick representation of $10 + 1 = 11$. The confident guy is just as surprised as the rest of the audience when I give my answer. "ZERO." I turn the equation upside down and go "Voilà!"

Maths has changed, our challenges are different, even the equation has changed. We are all now living in a world of exponential thinking and exponential change. It used to be stable, or at least we thought it was somewhat linear. What does that mean? If you go 30 linear steps, you will reach 30 meters (1,2,3,4...). But that was the old world. If you go exponentially, 1, 2, 4, 8, 16, 32, 64, you will travel 1 billion meters. This is the 21st Century – the age of exponential growth. Instead of reaching the corner of the street where you live, you will travel around the earth 26 times.

In 1439, German blacksmith Johan Gensfleisch, also known as Gutenberg, began work on the first moveable-type printing press (although the Chinese might have other thoughts on its origins). Even though more than 90% of the population could not read or write at that time, he thought it was a good idea to invent a printing press. And his invention kick-started an inexorable wave of human knowledge. Thanks to his creation, over the last 250 years we have left the churches, challenged the Bible, and disseminated information with ever-increasing speed and pervasiveness. I looked earlier at how a century ago it took 100 years to double the information available in the world, yet in the past year we created more information than we had throughout the history of mankind. Computers are outcompeting human beings and will replace around 2 billion of the 4 billion jobs we currently have on our planet. (Yes, math geniuses, that means HALF of all jobs!) But I am confident we will be just fine. We will come up with new solutions, as we always have, and may eventually get back precious time to do things that are engaging and fun. Wouldn't that be great? Go computation! Well, let's not get too carried away. There will be no dream scenario... but as I said, we will be fine.

Our brains are not wired to think exponentially. Instead, we align linearly and use the facts of the past to predict the future. For human beings, these things are difficult to grasp and to understand. Our brains are not wired to think like this. We are walking concoctions of flesh and blood, connected and wired with a bunch of destabilizing feelings and emotions. Numbers and statistics are dangerous stuff.

Statistical reasoning, the challenges we use to make predictions and doing risk analysis are what statistician and essayist Nassim Nicholas Taleb discusses in his books *Black Swan* and *Antifragile: Things That Gain from Disorder*. Taleb's non-technical writing style and his touch of philosophy have made him one of the most admired thinkers of modern times. Taleb states that some things (and some people) benefit from getting shocked. They thrive and grow when exposed to volatility, randomness, disorder and stressors, and they love adventure, risk and uncertainty. Yet, in spite of the ubiquity of this phenomenon, there is no word for the exact opposite of fragile. Taleb has called this concept "antifragile". Antifragility is beyond resilience or robustness. The resilient resists shocks and stays the same; the antifragile withstands them and gets better.

The Cognitive Reflection Test (CRT) was introduced in 2005 by Yale University psychology professor Dr. Shane Frederick. Its purpose was to demonstrate how rational we are. The questions asked in the CRT correlate to the subject's intelligence or IQ. The results show and measure how reflective the subjects' answers are of their mental state.

Dr. Fredrick's test initially contained just three simple questions. You can try them yourself; pull out a pen and write the answers down before moving to the next page:

1. A bat and a ball cost $1.10 in total. The bat costs $1.00 more than the ball. How much does the ball cost?
   _____ cents
2. If it takes 5 machines 5 minutes to make 5 widgets, how long would it take 100 machines to make 100 widgets?
   _____ minutes
3. In a lake, there is a patch of lily pads. Every day, the patch doubles in size. If it takes 48 days for the patch to cover the entire lake, how long would it take for the patch to cover half of the lake?
   _____ days

People who score high on the CRT are less vulnerable to various biases in thinking, including prospect theory. By the way, the answers to his questions are: 5 cents, 5 minutes, and 47 days... but I'm guessing you got all three right, right?

....

....

....

....

....

....

....

There are obviously multiple aspects to touch upon when thinking about maths, equations and numbers. The equation itself has changed; there's an entirely different kind of maths on the table in the business world. When you produce screaming, flashing advertisements for poor products, buy blog posts and look for attention wherever you can get it, you will not succeed. Marketing is dead. Favourable attention is an outcome of your marketplace awareness and the credibility you earn over time. You cannot push something onto customers. Old, worn-out sales and marketing maxims are being challenged. Charles Darwin knew and understood that. He hated the peacock because this stupid creature survived evolution against all odds; it was an oddity that did not possess any of the attributes related to "survival of the fittest". The peacock is a bird, but it cannot fly. It struts around squawking and yelling, trailing a ridiculously long tail. What is its purpose, we ask? But once the colors are up and he flashes his beauty, the peacock is extraordinary, he is sexy. Similarly, we need to draw awareness by being unique, being ourselves, being extraordinary. Then, along this journey, we will build credibility. The reward will be attention.

So, this is the equation: Awareness * Credibility = Attention

Let's speed it up.

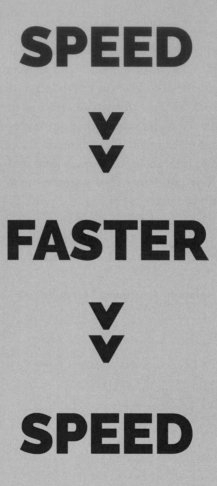

"Speed is often confused with insight. When I start running earlier than the others, I appear faster."

– Johan Cruyff

The Dutch footballer Johan Cruyff was actually right; speed is in many ways about knowledge, wisdom and data. But the problem today is that the speed is so head-spinning that if you are working on attributes, you should invest in speed. Adapting Darwinism to new circumstances at an ever-increasing velocity is inevitable. Once you have your focus and simplicity and understand the importance of execution, go for speed. In a world of chaos, rapid progress and change, seeming to have everything under control is, in fact, a sign of a problem. It shows that you simply are not moving fast enough, and you might be headed for a big shake-up. The lure of vicious wisdom lurks just around the corner. If you are not on the lookout for it, I can promise that you, the wise master, will be hit by an earthquake.

To avoid chaos, you need to know where you are going, and you need to be conscious of your decisions, your thinking and your focus. You may find yourself in a loop where you are continuously optimizing the decision-making process. Take a deep breath and inhale the air of chaos. Regardless of how we try to add mindfulness, deceleration and spirituality to our lives, the speed of change and the infinite revolution will not stop. The universe will continue to expand and the sun will shoot ahead at an ever-increasing speed. You cannot neglect speed, but you must respect it.

Entrepreneurs and businesses should invest in speed. Regardless of how much you focus, what you are good at or what you like, you need to invest in speed. Not big data, but *the right data* – for you, for everyone, in the right amount and at the right time. And make it fast! Today you need it all, and ideally, as technology has progressed, the information should be available to us before we even realize that we have a need for it.

As speed increases, frustration inevitably mounts with the realization that there is always a better decision that can be made. We fail fast, learn fast, fix fast. In this crazed milieu, striving for perfection will leave you discouraged. Instead, learn to value every good step you take and to love decisions that help you move in one direction. The perfect state is something we do not reach – the optimum can only come out of making subsequent good choices. Learn how to value these experiences and accept the reality of your bad choices, but fix them quickly. If you cannot make a simple and fast decision, chances are you do not decide at all. Speed is everything.

The pace is increasing, and we rely on existing knowledge to understand the change around us. We are constantly moving forward; there is no slowing down. Forget the promise of "once you get older you will have more time," as the only time you have is NOW, and this is what you can influence. Time is moving forward.

The major advances in the speed of communication and our ability to interact took place more than a century ago. The shift from sailing ships to using telegraphs was far more of a radical change than that from the telephone to emails. The speed of modern communication is wondrous to behold.

As the speed increases, we fool ourselves into believing that we can catch up, that science can shift into overdrive and surmount all obstacles, but there is no final station or destination. If we were, in fact, to figure out the world, the universe and the galaxies, then we might, through our superior skills at creating knowledge, explain it. Yet the reality in which we live – our Earth – is so tiny and does not symbolize any typical state in which we find ourselves. So, the solution to all of these problems lies in the speed of progress, through our use of technology. The path forward will, therefore, be an optimist's view of science and technology, outrunning the negative uses of the same technology. We have won this race over and over, but there is no guarantee that we will win again. Nor is there a valid, calculated probability of a destructive scenario. The advantage we have is that the prophecies of doom, these pessimistic and frustrated worldviews, are driven by facts. Whether found in belief systems, in religions or in the field of science, the pessimist will be convinced by the opposite with great difficulty. And this remains our driving force as we try to find sufficient speed for coming up with new solutions. Neither the irrational belief that the outcome will be ideal, nor that it will be disastrous, is reliably likely. And so, the debate goes on. It has led to the collapse of civilizations; they unfortunately, fatally, did not know enough. The progress of knowledge was not to their advantage.

So, the race continues, and the key factor is speed. It is theoretically and physically possible for us to fail at everything due to a lack of knowledge, meaning that we have not been fast enough to create knowledge and tame it. It may be possible to create some kind of global climate regulator, similar to how we use our indoor air-conditioning systems. Sure, in theory, but are we fast enough to come up with the knowledge necessary to do it? We will see. In the future, any challenge (danger) will inevitably be the unforeseen... and the solution will be wild knowledge.

Key events throughout history can be defined by the beliefs and convictions of the philosopher or thinker. These worldly events have one thing in common: they have happened at a quickening pace whilst corresponding advances in technology have engendered ever-increasing complexity. And as diversity becomes more diverse, complexity becomes more complex. We need to understand the impact of speed, yet we must also avoid many problems of the past that resulted from our exponential progress.

It is also important to work at controlling the speed. Forget the term "work-life balance" once and for all; it is outdated and from my perspective never really existed. There is no distinction between work and life. Everything is a part of your life, and you have to find a way to lead a life that is in balance. Even with the increasing speed and complexity of things, you are equipped with the conscious power to slow down and find your life-life balance. So the good news is that even though things seem crazier than ever, you are still in the driver's seat. You have a lot more power to control your life than you think you do. You can choose how to react, how to focus your time, and what to let go of to make your life simpler. You can try all the new productivity apps and tools, but it all boils down to your self-discipline and the choices you consciously make. It is about YOU and trusting yourself. It is about "The Now," combined with how you choose to interact with others.

TO-DO AND NOT TO-DO ...AND THEN TO DO

"True eloquence consists of saying all that should be said, and that only."

– Francois Rochefoucauld

In other words: "Say all that you need to… but nothing else, stupid!"

In a way, this also applies to what we should do versus what we could do. "We should do this," says the charismatic leader, and everyone obeys. This is classic top-down command and control. "We *could* do this," on the other hand, is aimed at getting others onboard. It is an opportunity to leverage and it is inclusive – things we can explore together, or *outside-in* versus *inside-out*. "Should do" very often has an expected outcome, while "could do" signals a journey in search of wild knowledge.

"Your most important questions are the ones you have not yet asked."

"There is nothing more complex in the twenty-first century than simplicity."

There is nothing more complex in the 21ˢᵗ Century than simplicity. Nothing is "simple" – when someone says this they are actually simplifying.

In a world where it feels like everything has already been invented and created, and every profound thought has been written, it may seem that there are no small secrets left to uncover. It appears that we are only left with the greatest mysteries. Mysteries such as "I", our mind and consciousness, and the infinite universe. The frustration of seeing a gap between ubiquitous commodities and things we might never be able to figure out is our daily struggle. And it feels like it is increasing. The good thing is that it has always been this way. Even during the initial years of "the Industrial revolution", at the close of the 19th Century, we thought we had peaked on innovation, creation and technological progress. In fact, we now know we have come a long way since then.

One way to tackle this is through innovation, or horizontal change – doing more of the same, only more efficiently, using slightly new methods. Another way is to keep going after the "secrets" – what I see as *real* change, vertical change. That is where we manage to combine new models with new technology, or find a completely new perception... a leap into a completely new and unorthodox way of seeing the world. Through our experiences we take a journey toward simplification and find the right focus. On this journey, we have no end in mind, no ultimate goal, and by using buzzwords such as "Industry 4.0" and "Digital Transformation" we are simplifying things to find the right mindset to cope with the progress and change we are experiencing.

We learn that thinking is about accumulating knowledge, but without focus and the ability to simplify it we will not know where or how we can use it.

Great philosophers of the past already challenged the linguistic expression of our thoughts. With modern science and neurophysiological research we are now able to analyze the cortex and map the thoughts coursing through a human mind... but we are still left with a lot of questions. Whether it's the genius of Wittgenstein or Spinoza or the progress of science, still the secrets of knowledge and the playfulness of the human mind escape us. We are left with uncertainty and mystery, which for many is frustrating but still the source of creation, progress and creativity. Perhaps Einstein's claim that he only had two authentic ideas, or Heidegger's assertion that exceptional thinkers only have one thought, might be an over-simplification of their own achievements, but we cannot rule out that there is wisdom in that notion.

So even with a basic understanding, we are still far from comprehending our creativity, or our subconscious thoughts and dreams. Psychology, the field of neuroscience and recent, exponential development in the worlds of AI, biology and cognitive science are making significant progress. Nonetheless, many believe we have not come much further than modern philosophy. In his book, *What is Called Thinking*, influential thinker Martin Heidegger stated: "What is most thought-provoking in these thought-provoking times is that we are still not thinking."

In the fantasy short story *Funes the Memorious*, by Argentine author Jorge Luis Borges, we meet Ireneo Funes, a peasant from Fray Bentos, Uruguay. After falling off his horse and hitting his head, Funes recovers consciousness and finds he has an incredible new skill – or perhaps the biggest curse ever – namely, remembering absolutely everything. On the one hand, the story raises unresolved questions about the potential of the human brain. On the other, it shows us the limitations of access to infinite knowledge, memories, thoughts and experiences. Borges reminds us that the initial step in thinking is to forget. In order to have the right focus and reach a state of simplicity, you have to forget.

Even a topic such as honesty, which is central to coveted attributes like trust and empathy, boils down to simplification. We can claim to be truly honest, but if the ancient Greek philosopher Diogenes of Sinope, founder of "the cynical philosophy", was still around, even he would probably still be searching for that elusive *honest man*. This does not mean we are (only) liars but that most of us carry our baggage within.

In the famous play *The Wild Duck*, by Norwegian writer Henrik Ibsen, one of the characters talks about "Livsløgner", which roughly translates to a lifelong lie. It is a story about people who don't live a genuine life, but one of self-deception and illusion. They can only identify with the outside world, their surroundings and false ideas about themselves. An "apostle of truth" appears and tries to force the absolute truth onto them, but it turns out the average man cannot live a happy life without these deep rooted lies and false perceptions of themselves. The message of the play is that we cannot survive without this simplification. The desire to build trust is obviously a core element of honesty, but in a broader sense these small, self-perpetuating lies encourage us to keep going. They are a part of our simplified reality and assure our progress.

Simplification through automation is nothing but pale, faded thinking. In our fast-paced world, we do not think. There are ways to demonstrate this. For example, if we were to hyper-analyze every move, every curve and every possibility in traffic, we would have chaos on the roads. In the same way, our expressions, knowledge and wisdom are "thoughtless". They arise intuitively, or through trained, experienced reflexes that are our subconscious, spontaneous response to an effect.

No great artist, painter or composer can express their vision, feelings or ideas in relation to their inner form of expression – these are all simplifications expressed through the art itself, and by having the right focus.

"I cannot express this in words" is something heard from a person in love, but also by poets and philosophers. Intuition, and feelings of intellectual or psychological states of mind, are limited by our words and languages. Therefore, our knowledge, which through some 200,000 years of human history made homo sapiens superior to other species, is somewhat limited. When the apes threw us out of the jungle and onto the savannahs, something happened in the way that we communicate that helped us to survive through interpersonal expression and to go on to evolve as a species. This, in turn, helped us form societies and, around 5,000 years ago, in Mesopotamia, gave us written language. With this breakthrough we had the ability to write, and the game-changing capacity to document and save information.

So often what is defined as "totality", absolutes or perfectionism are simply unfulfilled thoughts and dreams, an expressed abstraction similar to infinity. Emancipation, future projections, plans – whether routine or utopian – can never offer a guarantee. The probability of knowing can be on our side, the generalization seems to be universal, and our hope is tied to "what we know". But the game of hope, as we know, is a dangerous game to play, with but one guaranteed outcome: death. Even so, as futurist Ray Kurzweil notes, with immorality getting closer, that is now also up for debate.

In a world of permanent revolution and change the future will be improvised and you need the ability to judge which aspects of knowledge are applicable to business and life in general. The lure of vicious wisdom tempts you to unlearn, to choose an unthinking approach, to reach a deeper understanding, meaning or reason… or simply to find new and different solutions. This requires focus or merely a subjective, conscious realization of the now – a simplified worldview. Our subjective reality is built on simplification, and that is what makes it so complex for a computer to grasp concepts based on logic.

We create structures, boxes and categories to simplify our own perceived reality. Yet, our perception is the lens through which we see our world. As powerful and beautiful as our mind can be when changing perception and reveling in creation, we can feel frustrated when we have to cope with complexity. A new perception, a different view, a new path that is not based on our logical reasoning – this is why the right focus and the power of simplification make us superior and help us move forward.

We can argue about the world and simplify our overly complex understanding of it, but the truth is that from the day that we are born we are presented with a fictional version of reality. We are taught and shown to be something, but in the entirety of the world we are much less important and relevant than a snowflake fluttering to the ground in Røros (my hometown in Norway). To put it in the words of theoretical physicist Stephen Hawking, we are just living in "chemical scum". Self-proclaimed experts and leaders can learn a valuable lesson by consciously realizing this and watching the video of a TED Talk by Israeli quantum physicist David Deutsch. (The TED program's curators, and I, think it is perhaps the best Ted Talk ever.) Deutsch argues that as we strive to find answers to big questions in various fields, we must realize that while the two resources, energy and raw material are scarce (still), the third, knowledge, is unlimited – basically the more you use, the more you have.

In the field of philosophy, we can find profound teaching on: focus and simplicity; how to move to controlled wisdom within our own paradigm; and using structured knowledge, driven by the art of thinking, to support our structured mental state – our own world, our own reality.

One of the masters of simplification, the genius French philosopher François de La Rochefoucauld, takes us back to the 15th Century. He lived in a time when we thought information was limited and matter unlimited, where the art of philosophy could help one understand everything. La Rochefoucauld took a very different approach. Long before the perfect, 140-character "tweet", La Rochefoucauld wrote a book, *Maximes* (the Maxims), that was barely 60 pages long. This was extremely untypical at the time, when books were thick and difficult to read. He was the master of simplification and outlined everything in brief, perfectly crafted proverbs and aphorisms. La Rochefoucauld's book stands among the masterpieces of philosophy for its role in highlighting the power of structuring information through simplification.

"Affected simplicity is refined imposture," he wrote, meaning that faking simplicity is an attempt to deceive others by purporting to be someone or something that we are not.

In recent times, we have seen multiple examples of supposedly strong leaders, even if they may not have a message or a solution. Rather, they practise authority and act "important", as if that is the solution to the growing gap between what one feels one knows, and what one could know. Our generation can think back and remember the days when everything seemed so much easier. For instance, operating a television was the very definition of easy – one button and two options, "on or off". Life was so much better back then, right?

Maybe it is this feeling that leads so many people to go out and vote for new parties, untested politicians and dubious opinion-makers who offer only one message: "It was better how it was," or "Let's become great again."

With the flow of information accelerating at an exponential rate, we are racing toward what some describe as "perfect knowledge". To me that sounds like a tamed state of what I define as wild knowledge, and though it is tempting to believe this, I think we are far from it. Perfect knowledge is a simplification of what knowledge actually is. As someone who loves technology, physics and scientific progress, I am doubtful that we will successfully dissect the structures of our thoughts and find out how our minds operate. We are waking up a little bit dumber each day, adrift in waves of technological development and the sludge of information-overload. From purely a data standpoint, the taming of knowledge is doable with AI.

However, the taming of knowledge is only possible if we have an end state of knowledge – a totality – and if we understand what thoughts really are. But we do not, therefore we have no "end state". The understanding of thoughts and knowledge cannot be achieved without an unpredictable (and to me risky) outcome of tapping our minds into the machine. Instead we should try to master the simple piece-parts of complexity by focusing and simplifying, so that we can enjoy progress and not be frustrated by the speed of change. I believe that we should continue our development of AI, and bio-technological progress, to improve lives, but we should remain focused on distinguishing between man and machine from a mind and consciousness standpoint.

We all know that frustrating feeling of not being able to decide, but having all the knowledge can also remove the option of making decisions. The simplification, or should we say optimization, of the decision-making process was something Steve Jobs understood and pretty much outlined in the Apple journey since the launch of the original iPod. Jobs, a master of focus and simplicity, introduced a new kid on the block – an mp3 player with one button (a big round one), two colors (black and white) and two sizes (small and large). He understood the customer's needs, which led to unprecedented growth… and *understanding the customer's needs* became the new standard. Jobs' bold vision made Apple one of the most valuable companies in the world. In retrospect it is all so obvious: the single button, and later, swiping, brought a level of simplicity that even the smallest children could auto-didactically adapt to in seconds. And always, with the advent of new technology, new models emerge to work with them. Once adapted, though, we take the technology for granted and move on.

The problem lies somewhere else. Business people talk about "Customer Centricity" and "Customer Driven," but too few actually take the time to listen, to understand, and to adapt to users – to their customers. But customers are the ONLY ones who have the power to throw everyone, including top management, out of business. The problem is very often that we map old behavior and models to the new technology we're given. But technology in and of itself does not have a purpose, it does not disrupt industries. It is what we do with it, or better, what our customers WANT to do with it, that changes the game. This is what determines whether your business will be around tomorrow. Customers are hungry for the attention they feel they deserve. They want to be valued. Businesses can deliver on those expectations by making products or services simpler and more efficient, or by adding other value that makes life easier. Get it? Customer Focus is not something you just write about or talk about – it is something you actually do. Go out and listen to your customers; they might actually have something to say.

The smartphone that we now take for granted teaches us a valuable lesson in how use of technology evolves and how customers change and adapt. Just 30 years ago my father was carrying a $10,000 "car-phone" around in the trunk of his vehicle. The only thing he could do with this device was basically pick it up, dial a number and say the words, "I am in the car," after which he would have to recharge it for hours. It was a bulky, stupid invention that served no real purpose. And so, many leading tech companies thought that it was nothing more than a plaything for the rich. Today, of course, it seems like the smartphone has always been here and that we couldn't possibly live without it. This is what technology does to us.

As I was explaining to my eight-year-old daughter while she was watching TV and playing with her iPad, we also had the "Care Bears" on television back in the late '80s (don't blame me, I turned out OK), but we didn't have the internet, computers or smart-phones. She looked at me and said, "REALLY? So you only had iPads back then?" I laughed and said, "No honey, not even iPads." Even 20-year-olds today have difficulty relating to the world without a smartphone. We now spend more time with digital devices than we do sleeping; recent studies show that we spend 7-8 hours in the digital realm every day. That means we spend half of the time that we are awake doing something that was not even imaginable 20 years ago. It is obvious that this is having a huge impact on our lives and changing the way we live. As the pace of technological development quickens, I believe it will outpace other areas of human evolution. What supports us on this journey of change and creation is our ability to unlearn, unthink, forget, and sort information, impressions and experiences into mental models that we project onto the new world. We find ourselves in a state of permanent revolution and change. It can seem chaotic and unstructured, but being a radical optimist I believe that we will evolve with the technology. By using new technology and creating new models, I'm confident that we will find new solutions, new ways of structuring and simplifying our lives, and new ways to grow our businesses.

Simplicity is about power. Those with power tend to control what is important to them, by doing less of what doesn't matter to them and more of what does. It has been this way throughout history, and within our hierarchical structures, those with less power have always struggled and today, given that we are moving powers into algorithms, the challenges will increase.

What happens is that we are drawn to simplicity. We will join, follow, connect with and even obey those who give us a simple plan, a dream and a vision to help us become something bigger and better. This is a problem today, when populist ideas and ubiquitous digital media drive insecure human beings toward radical opinions. People feel pressured to act based on this top-down approach. We have come a long way since the dictator screaming his vision of a new world order over the radio, and I suppose we saw the internet as the solution to all our problems, in a stable, more liberalized world. But face it, we still have a way to go. The feeling of belonging and connecting is hard-wired, deep in the human mind, and because of this we do not consider or rationally evaluate the cause-and-effect power of the networks that we tap into. This is why people vote for politicians who merely complain and inspire hope for something different. This is why 30-year-olds, bubbling over with frustration, move out of their parents' houses and are willing to go to war for whatever cause their "leaders" put on the agenda. The internet does not have a soul or a purpose. It has not given us a more liberalized world, but rather a tragically dumbed-down one that – with the maelstrom of radical opinions that it delivers – blocks and negates information that would otherwise broaden our horizons.

At the same time, these platforms only reward similar opinions, so the momentum of storytelling, sharing and "liking" builds on these agendas. These networks offer no reward for understanding and changing opinions, no recompense for empathizing with the human being behind the avatar, no questioning of the information propagated across personal networks. For me, these networks lead to feelings of wisdom and learning without the underlying context and clarity. Donald Trump and ISIS are phenomena of these free-wheeling platforms.

Today, we should study the art of thinking – and tap into the capacities of the right side of our brains – to plumb the wellspring of intuition, holistic thinking, visualization, imagination and creativity. One of the biggest challenges we'll face in years to come will be the evolution of our species vis-à-vis the speed of change that we experience.

This also applies to the corporate world. There is a sweet spot between the levers of top-down control, the numbers and processes, and the "bullshit" of inefficient meetings and memos. Simplicity in business comes from using common sense and practising empathy. It should map to the underlying needs of those executing the tasks. We need to think backwards and start with the people, not with rigid corporate process. Today we need to have the right mindset, the right people on board, and an orientation toward the reality of continuous change.

True simplicity, however, also boils down to respect. How do you as a leader respect the time of others? How good are you at using their time and yours? How do you support them in the creation of new models, and structure wild knowledge to make it a driver of change from within? Having a vision and a strategy for moving in a united direction, establishing a creative, collaborative culture and meeting the forces of change head-on – that is the role of a leader in the modern enterprise.

The complexity of the world and the sea-change of globalization are vexing challenges to cope with. Breaking the interdependencies of a globalized world into simplified messages that people can relate to is not only the role of political leaders but also the challenge for leaders and managers in any organization. So before focusing solely on execution, action and speed, leaders should prioritize and find a value framework, sharpen focus and structure thoughts through dialogue and interaction. Focus and simplicity are really the keys to brilliance. Speed is essential, but the simplification of reality is what allows us to connect for a common business purpose. Albert Einstein might have been celebrated for many things, but this quote attributed to him is particularly spot on: "If you cannot explain it to a six-year-old, you do not understand it well enough." You need to break things down to something you and everyone else understands. That's a lesson all of us should heed in this hyper-complex world.

As a leader or an entrepreneur, if you do not work backwards from the needs of the PEOPLE – be they your customers or your employees – then you will never effectively exploit the competitive advantage of simplicity. It is not your view, but their view, that counts.

Narrowing focus and doing the right things will lead to progress, so you should do things that matter. Focus on things you can control and understand that this is only a subset of the things that matter. These small principles are the key to persevering through the struggles we face every day. Ideally, we can achieve our goals and deal with the continuous pressure to be productive, while staying healthy and fit and finding time for family, chores and a bit of leisure. How helpful it can be to find simplicity and peace amidst chaos, frustration and confusion. With so many overwhelming challenges, the key is really quite simple: focus. The ability to focus will allow us to create and progress in totally new ways, on the essential things, the things that matter most to us.

Countless management theories and books on productivity encourage you to set aside quality time in the morning to do the work that is most important to you. This approach includes an emphasis on long-term projects where you do not get an immediate payoff. If you don't take in the big-picture, with a birds-eye view, your daily calendar will always be too busy and your time will be eaten up by the "small stuff". Another advantage is that once you complete key tasks in the morning, you will be pleased with yourself for having tackled the "the important stuff", which frees up energy for the rest of the day.

With all of these big, radical changes, and calls for revolution, we often forget the power of just getting out and doing stuff. Work on a five-year plan, or deep thinking about visions and strategies, serve a purpose. They provide directional guidance – a compass, if you like. But progress comes from action; it is the result of simply doing stuff. There are NO straight lines. Life is not linear. One of the master proponents of execution, Tom Peters, claims that his only true learning dates back to 1960 and boils down to a simple truism: "Whomever tries the most things wins." No complex formula, no arcane theories – just start executing. For many, the ego stands in our way. When was the last time you made a fool of yourself? Can you laugh about stupid things you have done? Vulnerability is the birthplace of creation, innovation and progress, but it comes at a price. You have to let go and accept that you will do dumb things. The first try will never bring what you are aiming for. Understand that you will never reach your optimal capacity, that there are always things you could have done better. Accept that, and know that if you just get going – if you just do it – the learning will come, the wild knowledge will be found, and you will sidestep the roadblocks of vicious wisdom. Talk to people, exchange ideas and move forward, fully aware that you have no idea where you are heading or where you will end up.

So, as this section comes to an end and we recap what we should do, not do, do later, we understand that simplification is what we are working toward. Our focus, our thinking out loud, the structuring of our thoughts, the right degree of focus, handling the speed of change and the frantic pace of society – they're all necessarily in a world that is out of control. If it seems that the world is in control, you are probably not moving fast enough. The question remains: moving fast enough for what? We should stop taking ourselves so seriously. If you can laugh at yourself, stop being so self-important, and then sort out your mind, things will fall into place. If you can manage that, the outcome will be focus and simplification in all aspects of your life.

In the workspace, there are many reasons for wanting to do less, and that can lead you to grapple with what you should really be doing. This may be the thought underlying the "work-life balance" question, where work is important, but it's not everything. People need to focus on life outside of work and on exciting, extra-curricular topics. They need to make an impact, or strive for goals, and become the best at whatever they set out to do. Progress in that direction comes from making the conscious decision to do less. Finding the path of doing less does not make someone lazy; it allows a clear focus on what TO DO. Once this has been determined there is no flip-flopping back and forth. Doing less allows you to effectively take on the things that you have consciously set out TO DO.

HAVE FUN – TRY IT – NOW!

CHAPTER IV
VALUES &
EMOTIONS

Are you living by "the categorical imperatives"? Are you aiming to become "a Mensch"?

In 1785, German philosopher Immanuel Kant introduced a philosophy that can be defined as a way of evaluating all your motivations for action. In his *Groundwork for the Metaphysics of Morals*, Kant explained that you should "act only according to that maxim whereby you can, at the same time, will that it should become a universal law."

So, what are the values and the moral frameworks by which we live or run our companies? What role do emotions play in our business and personal lives in the 21st Century? We know that feelings are influenced by emotions and vice versa. How much of this can be replaced by technology, and how much is left for us to accomplish by just being a mensch? Alongside the progress of technology and science, the ideas and the understanding of simplicity are values and emotions, which individuals and businesses can learn and profit from the most. There's been a lot of talk about these matters recently – the heart of the company – and that is good, at least it's a beginning, but only a few companies really live it.

In this last section, we will take on a crucial consideration for the overall being, the other pillar of philosophy, "the art of life". From a business standpoint, this given knowledge and wisdom is there for everyone to take advantage of. Business can profit from "mastering the art of life" though we are still at a very early stage of this.

As mentioned earlier, Google spent a year of intensive analysis and data gathering, querying diverse groups of employees on what makes a high-performance team. The conclusion: productive team members make an effort to understand their peers, build relationships, and then try to make *themselves* understood. This can be summed up in two words: being nice.

Good leaders are not afraid of being nice. How many of you like to help other people? How many of you like to be nice? If you can answer these two questions with a yes, then you have a shot at being a leader. Or, better still, you are a leader.

Coping with values and emotions is another example of complexity in most businesses, and obviously in our life in general, as we try to achieve a satisfying "life-life balance". Technology is now a given; anything that can be digitized will be chewed up by "the machine" and made as efficient as it gets, while the cost of physical objects plunges toward zero in our "zero marginal cost society". Left behind, however, is (still) the human being, the human capital – the mensch. So the overriding focus on technology and digitization is not a guarantee. In the 21st Century, successful organizations effectively use technology to free up human potential. The new winners are the maximizers of empathy.

There have been many books about a conscious revolution, and about moving from jealousy toward admiration, a time of generosity or a "sharing economy". The 21st Century will inevitably be a time when we move forward together and learn about our feelings and emotions. We all have emotions and need to leverage this aspect of our humanity. That said, businesses are not yet ready to talk about spirituality, nor to name a chief empathy officer (one might suggest the CEO for that role), so we need to move fast *slowly*, and not risk handing all that we have over to technology. I believe it is necessary, if our species is to survive, that we keep these goals at the very top of our agenda.

Throughout history, from the Vikings to Mahatma Ghandi, storytelling has driven and inspired human emotions. It is hard to point out exactly what the Vikings or Gandhi left behind, but they are valued in different ways and remembered as some of the greatest people, and dare I say "brands", who ever lived. What is symbolic is the realness and the authenticity that, without logically explaining, we can relate to and share. This authenticity drives the progress and success of their stories. Our emotions, feelings, thoughts and ideas affect how we react, and how and why we buy products or services, though we often invent seemingly logical explanations to justify our emotions.

We are still learning to connect and adapt technology to build ecosystems and exploit new opportunities. At the core of these ecosystems lie extraordinary ideas and values, powerful messages that tap into our emotions. This is the soft part, the authenticity, what we call "being real". It is where we build trust and relationships, where we learn to connect, engage and inspire the special feeling a relationship gives us and those around us. It is our understanding of empathy, our road towards compassion and increased self-awareness.

The problem? Most of us are still living in a vacuum, or what I call "reaction mode". And paired with our seven-hour-a-day connection to the digital world (on average), we might even say that we have become digital zombies. Today, we change our principles, and go with whatever comes into our mind first. Our faster-paced world has led us to feel frustrated about our ever-dwindling sense of control and achievement. We all need our own individual values and a belief system that we can tap into. It is something that our emotions relate to and value. We are all a product of our chosen reactions from the past. Unfortunately, for many it takes an underlying experience for them to get to a point where they can reach a deep, profound state of consciousness... to tap into their emotions and values. This is the type of change that comes from deeper learning, versus change that is driven by outside factors. The difference is set in a profound framework of values.

What is your framework? Are you (still) driven by "the outside" – or do you have inner strength? Do you trust yourself fully? That is, are you being authentic – real? Or, in these terms, are you true to the roles you play? Searching for the one "authentic-self" is as useless as running around trying to find Santa Claus or the Easter Bunny. The mirroring of one-self, and an increasing awareness of the various roles we play, is how we can move closer to our own uniqueness, how we can be the best version of ourselves, how we can be extraordinary.

LET'S WORK ON EDUCATION FIRST

We talk a lot about educational systems, acquiring the right skills and preparing for the real world. It is a given that people are shaped and influenced by their grades in school. Many are still under the assumption that they are bad at something because they performed poorly in a particular subject in the classroom setting. We still believe that we are a reflection of how we have acted, and reacted, in the past. Instead, we need to become conscious of how we react to *the here and now*. We can benefit from focusing on how we "choose" our emotions. We can always hope and dream for something better, but we need to understand that a conscious now is all we can influence because it is all we have.

We can and should change our educational models. Young people need early training in social skills and moral frameworks. We must instil in them a sense of hyper-curiosity and then satisfy that craving with continuous-learning models, supported and driven by technology. R.I.P. old-school models that teach us how to tame metals, when in fact there are no longer jobs to be had as physical industry workers. How can dull schools with boring teachers compete with information-rich videos on every imaginable topic – captivating tutorials that can be watched online, at any time, at no cost? How effective is the mind-numbing classwork of old when compared with a riveting TED Talk? We must disrupt and destroy the school system, as it no longer serves a meaningful purpose. The time is coming when high school and university students around the world will ask why they're being forced into these tired old boxes when all the great lessons can be found on YouTube.

The new model – life-long continuous learning – will be different. I do not have the answer, as the questions are not raised yet, but I know it will be different. What are the skills needed tomorrow?

"When I was 5 years old, my mother always told me that happiness was the key to life. When I went to school, they asked me what I wanted to be

*when I grew up.
I wrote down
'happy'.
They told me I
didn't understand
the assignment,
and I told them
they didn't
understand life."*

– John Lennon

We need to take a fresh new look at our children and the educational system we feed them into. For the most part, we study, learn and grade things that society decided were important a century ago. And so, we find ourselves trying to solve complex new challenges using old, outdated models. Elite students are, by virtue of their pedigree, given elite entry to the corporate world. And though I value a good education, there is truly no correlation between education and becoming a successful entrepreneur or business leader. One might even say that the best business schools have lost out on many of the greatest business thinkers and entrepreneurs because of this biased "old school" view of what makes an exceptional business person.

Consider the broad base of people who have made a moderately decent living, those who would never have been considered by our elite universities, dropouts, or individuals who just don't conform to the norm. Some examples are Henry Ford, IKEA's Ingvar Kamprad, Charles Schwab, Richard Branson, William Hewlett of HP, and the late, great Steve Jobs. The list goes on to include actors, film producers, artists, political leaders and athletes. Their ranks include George Washington, Steven Spielberg, Walt Disney, Tommy Hilfiger, John Chambers of Cisco and inventors such as Thomas Edison, Alexander Graham Bell and Albert Einstein. In his book, *David & Goliath*, Malcolm Gladwell explains the phenomenon of underdogs turning disadvantages into advantages and gaining the upper hand. Our common sense teaches us that being conventionally disadvantaged can be a deal-breaker. Gladwell refers to the work of psychologists Robert and Elizabeth Bjork from the University of California, Los Angeles (UCLA), who through their Bjork Learning and Forgetting Lab have researched the application of cognitive psychology to enhance educational practice. Their work demonstrates that there are many incorrect assumptions about how we learn versus how we think we learn. Robert Bjork came up with the term "desirable difficulties" in 1994. The thought is that by introducing certain difficulties into the learning process, we can improve long-term retention of learned material. The researchers explored the application of desirable difficulties and found that, against all odds, many underdogs have built successful businesses and in fact made it to the very top of their fields.

Standardized tests only measure one kind of human intelligence and schools only cater to a few learning styles. We are starting to recognize this, and changes are occurring, but we still have a long way to go. One part is the challenge of making technology and digitization more human, in relation to a value system. We are making rapid progress with technology and, as I've alluded to, we will eventually be able to wire up our brains to access a totally new form of intelligence. But this is binary intelligence, not consciousness or thoughts. These technological advances will be significant, but at the same time we need to be able to understand the impact they will have. We need to focus on fixing the core and prepare for that world where we may eventually see a world where we may eventually see 4-digits or even 5-digits IQ scores measured. It will be essential, for the growth of our society, that our leaders (and, really, all human beings) are trained in the basic values of leaders (and human beings), from an early age. And we have to start now.

For me, giving my eight-year-old daughter access to technology – providing her with a smartphone, and giving her an email address and an apple ID – is not a problem. Not a problem, that is, as long as I take the time to help her understand that it is necessary to connect with others socially and that technology is just a part of life. She is not a digital native, or a millennial, or the denizen of a transfer-society (where property rights are literally up for grabs), but she is digital-born and connected. This framework of social intelligence and EQ is something that needs to be offered through the education system.

What we see today is extremism of a sort that is a technological (or internet) phenomenon. A lack of real, flesh & blood social belonging is counterbalanced by feelings of connection offered by these extreme networks. Technology can be used both positively and negatively; we need to get a better understanding of the social aspects of our lives that are impacted by technology and how we can and should live with this predicament. If not, we will all become dopamine junkies addicted to the virtual world. Already today we are seeing the increase in addiction with patterns similiar to heroin.

As arguably the last IQ generation, we must acknowledge the need to move toward and harness the real human capital: EQ. This is where we can immerse ourselves in "*nowism*" and enjoy what we do every day. This is where we build the ability to exploit wild knowledge and have the surroundings, the atmosphere, the cultures that are necessary to withstand the wildness. This is where you slow down, read, reflect and absorb learning into your daily consciousness. Let's go there.

THE CORE OF 3 EMPAHTY - SELF-AWARENESS & HONESTY

1. EMPATHY

There are various models for measuring personality and they can all be broken down into the factors, or characteristics, that everyone should practise. This is what I call "the core of 3". These three traits are the basis for growth and progress – individually, in your personal life, and as a leader in your company. Empathy is probably the most important attribute in the leadership toolbox. I often joke about women being born with it, and men having to look it up on Wikipedia. Whichever way it is acquired, empathy must be felt, understood and practised. Those who maximize empathy are life's winners. But where do we start?

Empathy is a difficult skill to master and it takes practice. Training oneself in empathy opens hidden potential for extraordinary results, progress and growth. However, it is not something that only leaders should focus on; it should be a priority for everyone in the organization.

It is a distinctly human ability. With empathy, we are able to understand the needs of other people, to understand and feel others' situations and predicaments. Yet, it is important to understand the difference between empathy and sympathy, and not mistake one for the other. With empathy, you can appreciate what someone else is going through; you feel it and you can offer the necessary support. If a leader can feel the needs of employees, then his or her acknowledgement and response will increase productivity, collaboration and eventually happiness and efficiency.

Doubt, shame and anxiety push managers, entrepreneurs and leaders into positions where they feel that they must fight. As a leader, you are supposed to be strong. You firmly believe you should know it all and show no sign of weaknesses. But, in fact, vulnerability is the birthplace of creation. And in today's society, there is already a strong movement toward a deeper understanding, beyond what we understand as empathy. That deeper sentiment is compassion. The fourteenth Dalai Lama, Tenzin Gyatso, has been famously quoted saying that capitalism is a working model, it only needs compassion. But compassion goes beyond empathy – it is a feeling among equals, not abstract pity for the wounded and destitute. In order to feel someone else's darkness, you must know your own darkness. But we as a people have a long way to go to achieve this, if this is in fact the goal. The compassion we see directed at our own life defines how we're capable of feeling for someone else. We all carry our own baggage, our own joy and sorrow, our own excitement and pain. If only other people would feel that – if only we could develop it – then we'd truly connect. In business, this leads to a higher sense of trust and yields room for creation, progress, change and what we call innovation… or creation through error and correction, failure and recovery.

I think we can do well by practising our own empathy and at the same time accepting that we are "failtastic", – able to state out loud, without trepidation, that we do not have all the answers.

In 2015 the advocacy group Lady Geek, which works to make technology more accessible, measured internal culture, CEO performance, ethics and social media presence among various big-name companies. It ranked Microsoft the highest, followed by Facebook, Tesla and Alphabet (Google). The group's Global Empathy Index measures "corporate empathy" and defines leadership competencies. It clearly shows that young (tech) companies score high, while large, old, hierarchical enterprises are in deep crisis.

It seems that empathic companies:
1. Value and care about their cultures.
2. Attract young talent through innovation and creation, and by a high acceptance of failure.
3. Celebrate their CEO (without a directive to do so that comes from the CEO).
4. Insist on transparency.
5. Sell their brand's backstory (where they come from and what they have gone through).

6. Listen between the lines (use social media empathetically, understanding that on the other side of the avatars there are human beings).
7. Listen to the "haters".
8. Have ethics as a boardroom priority.

The role of a leader is to form stable relationships by listening empathetically to others and understanding their personal paradigms. By doing so, a leader can contribute to and invest in their goals. It is not an easy skill to master, but when done correctly it has the potential to boost business results exponentially. Empathy can and must be trained. It is important to work with an ultimate goal in mind, and by implementing many small initiatives along the way you're certain to see significant change. When talking about empathy the crucial part is to start by breaking it down into something simple. Many small steps eventually lead to bigger things. You can choose your reaction to complaints and consciously feel the story of your company every day, and this can foster change throughout the organization. It is something that must be prioritized, and embraced, across the team. Everyone should understand that empathy is not a "soft skill", but rather a 21st Century quality that has significant commercial potential. I will repeat this, in capital letters:

EMPATHY IS NOT A "SOFT SKILL", BUT RATHER A 21st CENTURY QUALITY THAT HAS SIGNIFICANT COMMERCIAL POTENTIAL.

It is time to exploit this potential right now.

2. SELF-AWARENESS

In addition to empathy, leaders needs to reach a better understanding of oneself. They need to show conscious awareness of their own defects and shortcomings. A good leader in the 21st Century focuses on the needs of others, seeks and is open to feedback and criticism, and admits that he or she is not perfect. The CEO (or founder) of a company represents its vision and is central to the organization's success. A prime example is the visionary inventor and business magnate, Elon Musk. Musk shows humility and drive, and he persists in his dedication to making an impact and changing the world. Some narcissistic leaders can find their own following, but leaders who remain humble and down to earth are the ones who are widely loved and celebrated. Simply put, "People follow people they like."

We're often stuck in our own little world of pride and self-possession, but a good leader is the complete opposite. A good leader understands the concept of groundedness. In 1955, in his famous speech "Gelassenheit" (*Coolness*, or *Composure*), the German philosopher Martin Heidegger spoke about the human understanding of technology and how we connect. On a deeper level Heidegger's speech revealed that leadership is built around the core concept of being *down to earth* (what the Germans call *Bodenständigkeit*). But, can these words be relevant today, and adopted as an art for everyone in the 21st Century? Can it become Rock'n Roll and sexy? I believe so. But let's get back to self-awareness and Bodenständigkeit.

In simplified terms, keeping your feet on the ground and showing modesty are at the core of authentic humility. Taking essential learnings from admired thinkers of the past, and understanding the real essence of these sometimes "untranslatable" German words, is key to devising a workable philosophy for today's living.

Let's go back 2,600 years and listen to Thales of Miletus: gnothi seauton – "know thyself". We all need a regular self-auditing to become more aware of our own strengths and our own short comings.

"I am convinced that there is no essential work of the spirit that does not have its roots in an ordinary groundedness."

(eine ursprüngliche Bodenständigkeit)

– Martin Heidegger

3. HONESTY

Understanding empathy and increasing self-awareness are part of the equation, but they can't exist without honesty. Being honest is central to leading a happy life, and it constitutes the basis for trust and strong leadership. It is impossible to hide the truth nowadays, so go with honesty and embrace the transparent world.

We should acknowledge that we have come a long way with the help of Google, Facebook, Snowden and all the technology we have created. Nevertheless, we have to stop lying. In the business world, living the truth is particularly challenging in difficult situations. But in difficult times this becomes even more important. It builds trust, credibility and a positive reputation. In short: you need people to trust you. If you show honesty in challenging circumstances, then strong, long-lasting relationships will grow. Once people trust you they will stand behind you, in any situation. This applies to our work and our personal lives.

We must start by insisting on transparency. Even traditional companies with great products and services have difficulty being transparent. We instinctively lay low when bad things happen, and make the minimum possible disclosure. Strong, successful companies defy that instinct by communicating frequently during good times, and proactively revealing problems before they get out of hand. They manage potential earthquakes and even avoid the damage of aftershocks. The problem is, we become vulnerable... which we, as leaders, believe is the same as being weak. We have been taught that the boss should be strong and must not, under any circumstance, show faults or foibles. But this cannot be the case in times of co-creation, permanent revolution, relationship-building and change.

Corporate secrecy and trying to paint a perfect picture can actually harm a reputation and build tension between the façade and the actual situation. Covering up or "facelifting" uncomfortable truths is like trying to hide a volcano. Successful organizations publicly confront their problems and openly communicate underlying issues.

Successful companies believe that the customer can handle the truth and that the marketplace will reward openness and transparency. This is not only the formula for coping with customers and the media, but when applied internally it also creates a strong culture – one built on truth and honesty.

Recently, though, we have seen many examples of obfuscation and deceit in scandals that have convulsed the banking, investment and automotive sectors. The problem in almost all such cases has been that the board and management do everything in their power to bury the truth. Eventually, the coverup falls apart, the truth is revealed and the consequences are quite nasty. Trying to manipulate and hide something from the customer may help you in the short term. So nefariously manipulating a diesel engine to compete with an innovative new transportation technology would be the same as riding a Nanotyrannus – the Usain Bolt of the Late Cretaceous Period – when everyone else is driving a car. Ultimately, cheating and manipulating is counterproductive and leads not only to lack of trust but can also have a destructive effect in the long run. The dinosaurs died, and so will the manipulators and cheaters. Here's another relevant truism: People who speak the truth have an advantage, in that they do not have to remember everything they've said and struggle to keep their questionable stories straight, which can be exhausting.

So, simply put, learn to accept reality, stop lying, and go for honesty each and every time.

FINDING YOUR MANTRA

From a personal and professional standpoint, you should have your vision and strategy in place. You should know where you are going and have a plan to execute – targets, tasks, objectives and key results – and possess the tools and processes necessary to get you there. There are of course many tools that help companies manage the daily irritation of e-mails, presentations and spreadsheets. This is important, and is key to achieving operational excellence. Nonetheless, there should be something even more fundamental – defining or finding your mantra.

Zen Buddhism defines mantras as the "instruments of mind". Steve Jobs, who lived by his mantra, famously said: "Simplicity is ultimately a matter of the right focus. Simple can be harder than complex; you have to work hard to get your thinking clean to make it simple. But it is worth it in the end because once you get there, you can move mountains."

Business people spend an inordinate amount of time crafting complex mission statements that adorn flashy web pages as justification for their actions. They spend a lot of time and money to project a dazzling image to the outside world. What you should do instead is focus on the inside, by defining a mantra. Finding two or three words is ideally what you aim for – an affirmation that captures your higher purpose and what you stand for. The simpler you can define it, the more meaningful it will be. This mantra will serve as the perfect guidance in what you do, and maybe more importantly, what you will not do. Companies that can reach back to their basic values in times of trouble can (and will) bounce back stronger than ever. In finding your mantra, look for inspiring principles to live by, or principles that will inspire others to live better, fuller lives.

We need to have fun – life can become too serious too quickly. We need to be curious in order to become creative. Too often we get stuck in the rat race, overwhelmed by the tasks, chores, opportunities and distractions in our daily lives. If we are not consciously connected with our personal and professional goals, they may suffer, dragging us into a state of delusion and frustration. Overcoming the frustration and speed of the 21st Century is crucial for success and a positive outlook, and for efficiency and happiness. Just like a computer's operating system, you are a product of all the modules that have been installed during your life and career. Likewise, a company is a reflection of all the modules it comprises. A mantra helps to simplify the rules; it forms the guidelines to lead your life and manage your business. It equips you to overcome the challenges and conflicts that the world throws at you.

The biggest problem is sticking to resolutions in the face of difficulties. When there are challenges or distractions, and we do not reach our objectives, we start to feel ground-down and defeated. Yet in most cases, we are stronger and better than we give ourselves credit for. Our state of mind and consciousness tell us how to react. If we get distracted, we face that "Gut-Feeling-Short-Circuit" I described earlier. This is based on our past experiences and our core values. Our wisdom would normally lead us to make the right decision, but external influencers mislead us into choosing negatively, and that leaves us with a sense of doom and gloom.

Your chosen self-concept as a leader of your organization (and custodian of your own life) decides your destiny. Your limiting beliefs or negative self-awareness belongs to the past. The good thing is that it is never too late to change.

Regardless of the state we are in, we can outline and define our mantra to empower a strong and positive future – one rooted in creativity, efficiency and happiness.

Follow these steps to define your personal mantra:
1. Identify what holds you back or drags you down.
2. Make a list of three disappointments from the past year, and next to each of them write down what you now know you could have done to make them successful experiences.
3. Write out your new mental mantra as an affirmation that is consistent with the results you would like to achieve.

For example:
Disappointment – _____ .
Why it happened – _____ .
How you will change it – _____ .

Follow these steps to define your organization's mantra:

1. What are the top three achievements your organization can claim?
2. What did you and your team do to make them happen?
3. Write down short, single words, or a brief statement, that clearly described how you got there.

For instance:
What we/I achieved – _____ .
How we/I made it happen – _____ .
Why we/I did it – _____ .
Write down your mantra – _____ .

LETTING GO

Once you have clearly defined your mantra – something that you relate to – you can continue to create two or three words, or a simple declarative statement, that you or anyone else can relate to. Make it something positive and powerful that will guide you in setting smarter goals in the future. It must be an affirmative statement and should be in present tense. At times of struggle, or when clear focus is required, invoke the mantra to summon up the inner strength, skills and abilities necessary for the trials ahead.

The mantra is like a good story, and you are the storyteller for your organization. The more you repeat it, the stronger it gets. It communicates a powerful message, provides inspiration, and gives your organization a positive affirmation to relate to.

We all have the power to stop accepting the things that are holding us back or distracting us over the course of our journey. Groups and teams led by a positive mantra and inspiring thoughts are driven to higher success. We have seen this demonstrated on many occasions, with Steve Jobs being one brilliant example of a leader with a mantra. Do you have your mantra yet?

THE POWER OF NOW

There is no past, there is no future, we have only *now* – *well, at least what we can define as a conscious now, as the real moment, due to the processing of our sensatory experiences and lack of clear definition of what conciousnes really is, still escapes.* We invent history, and dream, and improvise our future, and let our past influence how we make our decisions in the present. Yes, there will be a future, but it is not predefined. These days, as we turn to social media far too often, we're blitzed with proclamations of how great all businesses seem to be running and how perfect everyone else's life seems to be. But no business, no life, is free of pain and sorrow, struggles and challenges. We can spend all our energy trying to avoid it. Or, we can learn how to live with our past, and manage our current situation. And we can reward ourselves for changing our mind set for the better, instead of senselessly collecting "likes" for being alike. When we are in "continuous execution mode" and stuck in the exhausting, competitive rat race, we self-create a lot of unnecessary problems. This is fueled by narcissism, and an addiction to what we define as "social", as we feverishly collect our thumbs-ups, smiley-face emojis and followers. We reflect on what has been and ponder what is to come. We paint a picture of our future, and as soon as we experience the first glimpse of success we scramble for the status and fawning recognition we've seen portrayed in the media or fabricated in our own ego. Our mind leaps past what we can actually influence, in the now. The challenge is to honor the moment; the more you do so, the more you leave your pain and sorrow behind... and only then can you finally let go of your ego.

One of the most celebrated books on this was written by one of the greatest contemporary thinkers and spiritual teachers, Eckart Tolle. In his book, *The Power of Now – A guide to Spiritual Enlightenment*, Tolle urges us to become conscious of these challenges. Spirituality is still difficult to relate to in the business world. However, it is an essential realm for all leaders, managers, entrepreneurs and human beings to understand. In a society where we struggle to find our purpose and continue to search for happiness, online and out in the physical world, Tolle teaches us our own individual importance. This is the book's opening line: "You are here to enable the divine purpose of the universe to unfold. That is how important you are!" He offers a world of opportunity and meaning, where we can reach a fully conscious state and to learn to enjoy the moment, the now.

This new state of consciousness, and a more enlightened humanity, are needed remedies to the rapid pace of technological and scientific progress. Though technology seems to have changed us, the bigger and deeper changes to our species are yet to come. Unfortunately, due to the complexity of these interdependent times, many have been left outside of the connected world. Those left behind have been robbed of key insight and perspective on life and our far-flung, globalized world. It is the responsibility of leaders, organizations – and in fact every one of us – to support people and help them to grow.

Another thing to examine is the constant pressure to *be something*, something that is evaluated by others. Today we need uniqueness and difference, but the true experience of progress comes from finding an authentic you. There is no better you than you. And while many turn toward their religious beliefs, I would assert that there is no bearded man sitting up in the sky to whom we can send little messages. Baruch (Benedict) Spinoza, the eminent Dutch philosopher, told us this 350 years ago, and Nietzsche repeated it with his assertion that "God is dead." Your future is an outcome of your conscious decisions in this particular moment, in the now. A reliable psychological path on our road to success and happiness is to start removing the things that are dragging us down, eating up our energy or holding us back.

We experience the distraction and the frustration of not being conscious and present every day. Our spouses remind us, on a regular basis, that we are not listening. Only when we are conscious and in the moment can we truly listen, feel empathy and become credible leaders through the development of meaningful relationships. Whether it is surrendering to the moment, leaving your analytical mind and your ego behind, embracing your true self, showing empathy, earning trust or being authentic – while banishing uncertainty, frustration and fear – success requires conscious practice.

Many see these topics as esoteric, but having a clear mind is the basic price of admission for all leaders and entrepreneurs in the 21st Century. It is not about becoming a spiritual teacher, but about growing as a leader, as a mentor, and coping with the challenges of our times. With a clear mind and an orientation toward the now, the clarity necessary for sorting and understanding our thoughts becomes much easier to come by.

REALISM
RELATIONISM
THE NETWORK

"*I suppose leadership at one time meant muscles, but today it means getting along with people.*"

– Mohandas K. Gandhi

Working together to find the why, but also the *why not*, will help solve problems and get us to a better place. There is a strong global interdependency emerging; we are all connected. Can you feel how connected we are? Can you see it? This is the challenge, but we do not really understand what it means or how it will impact us. The values and emotions. The ethics that will guide us. The speed of the "Good Guys" versus the speed of the "Bad Guys", all of whom have access to the same opportunities and technologies. It is all there. You have to let go and accept that you are now a "we". You are a part of the totality, yet conversationally you obviously still get to use the subject "I" – the vital self-identifier that really makes you unique. The Individual is dead; young people today are now individuals in one, living a primary role in the connected society and exploiting connections and cultures of participation and co-creation in their secondary, physical world. And along with that, onto the scrap-heap of history goes "individualism".

INIVIDUALISM IS DEAD

A customer-centric focus (e.g., what is best for the people) remains the elusive goal we must narrow it down to. But even that has become more convoluted as we evolve from being complex individuals to simpler, more connected de-viduals. We all have our narcissistic inner voices looking for ways to promote ourselves… but since everyone is given the spotlight of the internet, the complexity and frustration increases, prompting us to seek simpler ways of organizing our lives. We cannot spend all the hours in the day liking each other's images in order to attract more followers. Our focus must switch to what we can create together as a group, where we as human beings become the simple bricks that build a masterpiece. With the rise of social media, we have found ways to supercharge our egos through technology. Everyone gets their stage and can perform – and become famous – overnight. The cost of posting thoughts on the web is "zero". Obviously, if everyone is on stage, no one is listening. Today we still need to be equipped with skills to "pitch", to "convince" and to "serve" other people, but the information must be unique and relevant to a particular person or audience. The real network boils down to the simple truth of real relationships and extraordinary content/performance. Content must be unique.

In coming years, we will learn to value uniqueness beyond the selfie culture we celebrate today. We saw the rise and fall of MyS-pace, where all artists were given the opportunity to become stars in the music industry. With each new technology, there are early movers who burst upon the scene and become experts, build huge sounding boards, and connect with large numbers of people. They have the simplest form of power: a network. If you do not have it, though, there are still ways to amass an audience. What are you good at, what will other people listen to? How can you refine and simplify your message and make it unique? The concept of MyS-pace also applies to Instagram. We all know the scenario, where millions of people set the scene, edit, filter and round it off with a tagline like, "Just a quick snapshot of myself." The sad truth for mankind is that most of these pictures are never seen, or they are only seen and liked by people expecting the same behavior they're engaged in. Colleagues checking in when they are in airport business lounges, shooting selfies, uploading perfect food images or the vacation shots from their "perfect lives". Ten years from now we will laugh at this behavior – at our pitiful "social-selfie society" – as we begin to understand a meaningful new purpose for social media.

WE ALL CARRY A RESPONSIBILITY

The connected person, through his or her network, holds the key to success. Choosing dialogue and being socially connected can help build trust and foster real, enduring relationships. Individualism is dead, and we are seeing the final aftershocks of its impact on our society.

We have seen it in recent time with ISIS, the large audiences cheering for Donald Trump, and other extreme political movements. These people are ignorant of the real impact and challenges of technology and globalization. For these reasons they are open to individuals and groups that offer some kind of status and social connection. To challenge this we need a new approach – a revolution, if you like – in our systems. Instead of learning about outdated models, studying old history and reading the same books we have been consuming for the past 150 years, the system must be realigned toward values, trust, respect, empathy and emotions. It must equip children with social skills in a world where physical space has become secondary to the virtual expanse of the internet. We also have a responsibility to challenge what we are told. Today the pressure to make money by maximizing clicks and views outweighs the value of information itself, and that devalues information's impact on society.

The march of technology has long left mankind behind, and our evolution is too slow to keep up. If we are to work within this construct, then organizations and their leaders need to understand that productivity, happiness and success come from a conscious way of living and doing business. Here, the basis is a strong, fundamental, value-based structure where we somehow "tame" technology to assure that the mensch is not left behind. And, we obviously do not want to allow rampant technology to kill off humanity altogether. Leaders must pair how the organization breathes and feels with a passion for going after the core vision. Above all else there should be a value framework that builds on empathy and trust, leaving vulnerability and shame behind. This way, the leader and the organization can enjoy creativity, progress, productivity, efficiency and happiness. The good thing is that we are on the right track and, little by little, we are improving.

With the death of the social-selfie society and the devolution of individualism, we will slowly dethrone the little Napoleons and the bare-chested Putins. Organizations with patriarchal structures – every hospital with a self-proclaimed font of knowledge called "The Doctor" – will be removed. The desk-pounding bosses in their corner offices will disappear as we stop listening to them. This might even impact how we see rock stars and celebrity soccer players, as we begin to revere the team and the group instead of the cult of the individual.

We are moving toward participatory cultures and a society where co-creation and working together are the only true formula for success. With this comes a huge change to companies and organizations of all types. It is not about the "I", it is all about the "we". Being a puzzle piece, or a Lego block, means being part of a bigger whole.

Gandhi used non-violent means to achieve his goals and viewed the human spirit as infinitely more powerful than the deadliest of weapons. Digital networks and the technologies that enable them have become more powerful than a 9mm handgun or a colossal ego. Successful leaders and their organization understand what it means to be interdependent and connected. The best leaders will recognize that traits like character, integrity and the ability to care and connect are what will influence employees. Just like the beloved Stephen R. Covey taught us with his *7 Habits of Highly Effective People*, we must embody the Win-Win mentality. It is an attitude that will help forge solid relationships, build mutual trust and deliver long-term benefits for all involved. Collectives, after all, are capable of achieving what a lone individual, toiling away in isolation, simply cannot.

A NOTE ON SOCIAL MEDIA

With the rise of pervasive digital channels, we can now name, rate, compare, shame, and rant and rave about brands in an open place. This scares many organizations, and they distrust this transparency, failing to see the positive impact these channels might have. But strong leaders will use these channels empathetically. They can serve as a forum where we can remove our masks and show our human face. They provide a space for dialogue, for delivering authentic, human messages. Companies that understand that these are platforms for empathy position themselves for succeess. This must start at the top and go through the whole organization. As stated earlier, the "social media" today has been built around narcissism and is not social. As we evolve, we will (hopefully) see that we need to find ways to reward open discussions, and change in opinions, and that we need to create real social models. As for media, the capitalistic model strives for clicks and shares and therefore only promotes extreme and rapid opinions, which obviously contradicts with "social". Today we're seeing CEOs of the largest corporations personally engaged with their companies' social media accounts, and that's a good start. If they can be honest and open and lead the way, we might be on to something.

LISTEN CAREFULLY; I WILL WRITE THIS ONLY ONCE

In business, I still see many managers do nothing but talk, talk, talk. Meetings start with the CEO's views on everything. People get distracted, tune out and end up feeling lost and helpless. Still, the boss rambles on. Today we live in an action and attention economy. All we do is consume the time of others, in an age when the attention span of a goldfish is greater than that of a human being. It's true! According to statisticbrain.com, recent studies show that in the year 2000 we were able to focus our attention for 12 seconds, but by 2015 that had dropped to just 8.25 seconds. Meanwhile, the attention span of the humble goldfish has remained steady at 9 seconds.

A real leader practices "Giraffe Language", a concept otherwise known as compassionate communication. Giraffe Language helps us to speak from the heart, to talk about what is going on without judging others. The giraffe has the largest heart of any land animal, and it has two really big ears, which kind of tells us that we should listen twice as much as we speak (since we are equipped with two ears and only one mouth). The long neck of the giraffe is a characteristic that symbolizes the distance between the head, the mouth, the ears and the heart. We also know that a gut-feeling comes from both our mind and our heart. So, metaphorically, a long neck gives one more time to respond thoughtfully, as opposed to being in knee-jerk/reactive mode. The problem is that we tend to listen in order to reply, not to understand. This is something we can all think about the next time we formulate a snap-judgement, and are tempted to deliver a shoot-from-the-hip response.

A real leader spends time listening to the concerns of the team – to its members' views, ideas, wants, needs and problems. Build a reputation for listening. As a leader, you will be amazed how influential listening can be (as opposed to incessantly talking, talking, talking). In our "oh so complex world" the answers are often right in front of us... we just need to listen and be conscious of them.

A FINAL
SECRET:
SHARE

Stay foolish, stay playful (Disney, Steve Jobs, Pixar) and share – you have to be able to let go. Stop being so self-important! Engage in active listening by repeating people's words back to them and mirroring their emotions. You must share your experience and help structure their thought processes.

Success is sweetest when it is shared – when you have all the winners around you, and together you revel in the joy of the moment. Better people than yourself can, in fact, contribute greatly to your end-result. Do not be afraid to hire them. Finding people who share your passion can be beneficial, even necessary, in the quest to realize your goals.

THE
COMPANY
HEART

"The business of business boils down to one word: MENSCH."

The heart of any organization is its culture – the collective essence that it is impossible to copy. If it is strong and sufficiently nurtured, your culture can be what helps you get through trying times. Your culture is created by you, by your employees and by your customers. Building a strong heart is an ongoing, 24/7 activity. While technology is a force pushing you from the outside, you need to have the right mindset to direct you from the inside. We are thinking and acting organizations, consciously following our purpose and values. And although purpose and values reside at the epicenter of your organization, it is the heart that helps it to breathe. It gives us a higher meaning, access to playfulness, a lifeline to happiness, and it provides guidance when we move, like a compass in stormy weather. One of the most celebrated books on the topic, *True North*, by Bill George, gives us deeper insight into why and how this influences our business, and how it can guide us as individuals. Even more so on a personal level, we are driven and guided by the wisdom of the heart.

Screw the mission statement, and simply describe who you are. Your vision comes from the heart, and, as we talked about earlier, from carrying a mantra. You need to let people know what success will look like when they reach it – give them a snapshot of the future. Passion for a vision is contagious. Putting your heart into it, and defining it in the language of the heart, that's how you compel those around you to buy into a vision. Customers and colleagues get engaged when they see you do and say what needs to be said and done to make your vision a reality. We must lead with a vision for something in the long term – and we must lead with our heart – to find our destiny. Do you have the courage to follow your destiny? As described by Simon Sinek in his book, *Start with Why*, you must understand that people don't buy what you do, they buy why you do it. Excited employees and customers who believe in your cause are the most powerful resources any company can have. As with the heart, it is not something you just fabricate and layer on like a coat of paint; you just have it. Companies don't have culture, they *are* the culture – this is their essence.

But what would the perfect company culture (company heart) look like? Ideally, employees should love their work, or learn to love it, through the environment, mindset and setting. They enjoy going to the office, and their formal business hours become inconsequential. They do not spend their time watching the clock.

A STRONG HEART COMES FROM STRONG PEOPLE

How many valuable relationships can you count in your company, bonds with people who envision a future that is real and enduring? This is where you need to invest your time wisely.

You also need to understand that you need good people – no, *great* people – around you. Many managers are afraid to hire better people than themselves, out of fear that in the presence of star performers they will be seen as replaceable.

Great leaders and entrepreneurs do the opposite. They either hire better than themselves or train people to become better. Also key are matters of attitude and readiness. Investors and customers want to work with good teams that have a proven track record, but just as important is hiring talented but unproven people who are hungry for validation. Those around you will appreciate that you value talented people who are excited about being part of a collaborative team. In short, you must be willing to abdicate your throne.

In the old world, you sucked up to the people at the top. Now, because of how we communicate digitally – "nobody" is the new "somebody" – you should sow many seeds and let these people find you.

BUILDING AN ETHICAL HEART
– A BOARDROOM PRIORITY

The organization of the 21st Century is a house of glass – through social media channels, the innermost aspects of your company are now visible to all. What we had defined as our "private space" is shrinking daily. Expect and understand that everyone is interested in how you operate, which partners you're engaged with, what it's like to work for you, and so on. Everyone else's problems are now your problems too, and they can spread like wildfire. All organizations and brands need to define their ethical heart. There should be people on the board asking, "Should we do it?" instead of just "Can we do it?" Volkswagen, with its recent emissions reporting scandal, is a great example of that. Every hidden secret will eventually reach the light of day and will cause much greater damage than if the company had faced down its challenges in other, more difficult ways. In today's public interest environment, there are no hidden secrets... or if there are, they won't stay buried for long. Therefore, taking an ethical approach to the values of the brand, and the organization, must start in the boardroom.

How would you define your company's heart?

LIVE (LOVE) IT OR LEAVE IT

Let's be honest, no one can bring the same passion and focus to the table every day. But we can train our consciousness. Even Socrates used to sing at night; he sought the "art of life" and understood joy and playfulness. What if you woke up tomorrow and were asked to describe your life? I think all I would say is that it did not turn out as I'd thought it would. A hundred years ago, our lives were more predictable: we worked to provide for our family, and peoples' lives were more linear – arguably more stable. Then we started to play with technology and found ourselves flying across borders, which accelerated the pace of urbanization and of globalization.

So, is it really all based on serendipity? How many days do you manage to say that you are living the life you wanted or planned for? Write down what you want over the course of the year ahead, or start with your hopes for the coming week. What will you find? What would it take for you to get a clear picture of yourself? It's quite simple, really. You just have to do it. Paint the picture and then take action, for you have the power to make it so.

BE HUMBLE – BE INTERESTED – BE INTERESTING

Let your team know that you are always in learning mode. There is something very real and appealing about leaders who admit they do not know everything and are looking for answers. If you are interested, you will become interesting. People admire mentors and follow leaders who listen and can actually learn a thing or two from the little guy.

Have a clear vision of where you want things to go, articulate it passionately, and then set an example by taking action to make it a reality. Feel where you want to go and be real in the way you communicate it. You must live the life you choose; you must live your relationships, your company, your career.

WHAT'S WITH LOVE THEN?

Motivational speakers and all kinds of start-up conferences teach you about feeling the love – you have to love what you do. Otherwise, we're told, you might as well leave it for something else. As Steve Jobs said in his Stanford commencement address, "The only way to do great work is to love what you do. If you haven't found it yet, keep looking. Don't settle." We often get this wrong. "Keep looking" Jobs said. "You are making your money out of motivating other people and you are good at that, and eventually not only live it but also love it. You are the dreams and hope and passionate about tomorrow (e.g., start-ups) or you are a giant with all the experience you have made."

I don't think finding love is a prerequisite for starting a business or building a fulfilling career, let alone doing great work. In fact, I think it's disingenuous for really successful people to put so much of the focus on love, just as it's deceitful for the rich to say money doesn't matter. People tend to romanticize their own motivations and histories. They value what matters to them now, and forget what really mattered to them when they started. It's human nature; this rewriting of personal backstories is something we are quite good at.

Many innovations (and great businesses) are not born out of love, but out of frustration or even anger. Today, the early-movers are often young people who dive head-first into an area they are frustrated with. One example was the music-sharing service Napster. The big music companies started throwing lawyers at this young upstart, which was obviously a stupid, shortsighted idea. In response to the corporate pushback, countless successful new business models emerged. A prime example is Spotify, where you can access some 30 million songs. Today, large-scale file-sharing is yet another technology/product/service that we love and take for granted. Travis Kalanick and Garrett Camp, the co-founders of Uber, didn't start their ride-sharing service because they were infatuated with transportation or logistics. They started it because they were sick and tired of not being able to get a cab. It may be that Kalanick and Camp love running Uber today, but this game-changing company grew out of two young peoples' dissatisfaction with the way things were. But, again, this describes only the simplicity of the business models, and the good thing is that this is only one side of the coin. With an organization built on the values of Kalanick, the company will face other challenges in our changing world. Although we are not there yet, to have a human-capitalistic model, growth on behalf of any human aspect is not healthy and will be punished. From my stand-point, either Uber adapts or finds someone else at "the top", or it will eventually be replaced with another player. The simple business model though, is here to stay.

If you ask, many successful entrepreneurs will tell you that they do not always love what they do. Innovators, creators or technical geniuses can become stuck in the corporate life of meetings and reports and all the responsibilities that come with running a growing organization. Most of them choose to do exactly what they do, and would not change it for anything in the world. Many have found ways to love their organization and everything that goes with it. But love is not a prerequisite. In the long run, working with great people, building strong teams and nurturing deeply productive relationships is what they value the most. If it's there to begin with, the love will shine through in what you do and it will grow stronger. The point is that you can get out of bed every morning and be intrinsically motivated, with a good feeling about what you are doing. As Steve Jobs said, "If not, keep on searching." The love – if it is there, and if it grows and deepens – is a bonus.

Just as Uber was once the stuff of a brainstorming session, driven by frustration, that grew into a multibillion-dollar company, many entrepreneurs started their companies based on a desire to improve upon what previously existed. Frustration with the old way of doing things is the driving force, and it can eventually lead to something we love. Legal advice (lawyers), medical advice (doctors), investment advice (bankers) – there are still many fields that frustrate us, when in fact they should be all about making our lives better. Face it… if you don't change it, someone else will.

These are not definitive answers to questions you may have; I have not given you a fool-proof recipe for happiness and success. With these chapters, though, my intent has been to impact how you think, to trigger new questions that reveal answers for you and your organization. The world of wild knowledge will not be tamed any time soon, and that opens the door to a world of possibilities. Not fear, not frustration, but opportunity.

As you close this book you should realize how special this is, and what it means to be a mensch. The opposite of an "unmensch". You should reflect about your ideas and how to start doing, potentially with a group of people with different mindsets than yourself. In our new reality, you need to master the simplification game, bring practical philosophy into your business world and your life, and enjoy values and emotions and the progress that comes from a better understanding of one self.

Enjoy it now; tomorrow you will have lost another day.

#beamensch

CHAPTER V
OUTTHINK THE REVOLUTION
A (BUSINESS)
PHILOSOPHICAL
OUTRO

The world has changed, we are told what to eat, how to vote, what to say, what to think, as a result we do not think for ourselves. We are entering a new era of Philosophy. We are at a time of change, time of crisis, time of unlimited opportunity, time of rebellions, time of normality and abnormality, time of difference, diversity, alternative solutions and creativity. However, change will not come from the top, no politician, no leader; no individual will be the change maker. It is the era of the mensch, the beginning of infinity and permanent revolution and improvisation moving towards infinite knowledge and change. Philosophy, how it was intended to be, when Socrates first taught Plato and Aristotle, will guide us through the times of change. Today philosophers are needed everywhere and are soon to be found on the payroll of any organization.

Capitalism is dead, our educational system is broken as we are still educating industrial workers, and our political party serves two sides; one, the pseudo democratic value-system and the other, the populists ('Populism' originating from the Latin word meaning 'for people') – It is messed up. Our ability to reflect and think are over-shadowed by the powers of populism from ISIS to Brexit to Trump, all outcomes of technology, the internet, artificial technology, driven by forces underneath the elite of finance and self-proclaimed leaders. The problem is not the politicians and the leaders, but the system, which forces these people to the top, even though they are not intended to be there. But we can do better, and we will.

PRACTICAL PHILOSOPHY

We can divide Philosophy in two pillars, the art of living and the art of thinking, and I am confident Philosophy will also guide us in the path to cleaning up our lives. Searching for happiness is the wrong state to be in, we should always be aiming for fewer problems and struggles and spend less time being unhappy, and serve "Genügsamkeit". Throughout the years, never have we had more available to us, yet the resolutions for every new year aim higher. Let go of things that are dragging you down or holding you, your career or your company back. It is like cleaning the stairs, only in life you start at the bottom, and try to move to the top.

Will we live more ethical lives? I am not a spiritual person, and yet I believe the concepts and the practices of living a more ethical life are useful. They are useful in the context of philosophy and of our understanding of consciousness and our human mind. At first we may get freaked out by terminologies such as "mysticism" (mystical), "spirituality" and "transcendence", but these words are slowly moving into our (business-) lives. The problem is us. with our our ordinary experiences; and maybe this is what Norwegian Novelist, Karl Ove Knausgaard means when he, *The Alchemist Of*

The Ordinary, states that our ordinary life is full of invisible things that are dramatic. It is hard to describe such matters in words, but it describes the situation and the challenges – just as new terminologies in technology and science have found their place in our lives – the terms around spirituality and transcendence I believe will too. We have our (justified, from my personal view point) doubts about religion. We are exploiting on the subjectivity of religion as we move to a crossing of science and spirituality. Some will exploit this and test it (all). Be it the old models or new-age preachers of modern terminologies choosing a Yogi path and related rituals, or the Avant-Gardists exploiting on various drugs and substances, pilgrimage or spiritual enlightenment (omniscient) test it on your own life, find new ways to describe it. As we learn how to apply practical philosophy in our businesses and our lives we will learn how to slowly move towards these awkward terminologies and eventually take them for granted, however before that it is the second pillar, "the art of thinking" we must focus on.

RE-DISCOVERING THE ART OF THINKING

Something has gone fundamentally wrong, economy and business both need philosophy, and philosophy needs business. For decades, managers and leaders have been taught to be strong, self-secure, confident, and experts, omniscience, show no weakness. In the 21st Century we are seeing the lights of humility, modesty and frugality. It is not that we know something, or know it all, but furthermore that we accept and know that we know very little.

Let's turn away from illusions of infinite financial growth and the unlimited realization of all our materialistic dreams. I do not mean that we should say good-bye to having goals and to hard work, but rather that we should aim for maximized profitability and short term growth.

In fact we are already returning to Agora in old Greece where Business and Academia lived hand-in-hand. The dialogues of Plato and the simplification of Aristotle. A balance between the intellect, the emotions and the spiritual. But media paints a different picture, as taken up in various examples throughout the book. Everywhere we look, there is dynamic, and at times frustration is growing. We search and see the things on the surface level, and the pressure to control everything is tearing us apart. We move to cities to exploit countless possibilities, but the more information and open doors we have in front of us, the less we seem to come up with the answers. If we look at the year 2016, we know that some progress and achievements were made, but by media accounts 2016 was defined as a terrible year. The Americas are now free of measles, a disease that killed 200 million people, WHO declared the terrible Ebola virus to be over, according to the Global Terrorism Index there was a decrease in deaths of 10%; acidic pollution is back at levels equivalent to those measured in the 1930s; and the CO2 levels (although we still need to reduce this) were flat for the third consecutive year; after peace was declared in Columbia the Americas are now a content of peace; and wars in general are a quarter as deadly as the wars experienced in the 1980s and 100 million people rose out of extreme poverty (that is 3 people per second). So, this is it, the perception of how we see the world. We are now left with re-discovering the lost art of thinking and the skills to exploit our wild knowledge. R.I.P. Prof Hans Roßling, we will all carry on your dream of a fact-based worldview.

The Philosophy of Philosophy, brings us back to basics, to finding the skills required to reflect and to question the state that we are in, and to accept that we do not have all the answers, and therefore search for new questions. We understand the interdependency of our world today, that we can only manage the challenges ahead together. We are all the Lego pieces, we are all participating, fulfilling the totality of a presumed and envisioned masterpiece.

The lost art of thinking and philosophy is your loyal companion through the journey of constant change, a guard railing, a missing link and connector between efficiency, hyper-competition and creation – and a warrantor for challenging and questioning the status quo. With the ever-increasing complexity in our search for simplicity, the given models are not sufficient.

Our analysis of the mind is progressing at a rapid pace, we are chasing the thought and the consciousness. Although progress has been made, and new discoveries have been found through splitting the left and the right half, and various experiments of reverse-engineering in each and every corner, the real definition of consciousness still escapes. All we have is what we define as a conscious now – the real moment – due to the processing of our sensory experiences.

We must continue to ask questions and critically reflect on various aspects of business and doing business, and then come to a deeper understanding of what business is, what having knowledge delivers, and what roll business plays in other fields and societies. We must continue to seek plausible explanations and find questions in science, in philosophy and continue our journey of technology. In order to do so, we need the critical analytic mind that challenges the answers and discovers the external influencers. The CEO, and with him the whole organization, needs practical philosophy. A re-birth, if you like, of a clear mind, because we need questions, not answers – we have them all. What we need is to master the art of thinking clearly and rediscover the art – yes the art – of making money.

THE WORLD
AHEAD

So, what is going on in business today, where are organizations headed, what will this new world be like, and what will we need to learn in order to adapt? Throughout history we have only been able to guess and create using the elementary monkey logic that we are equipped with.

THE BEAUTY OF CASH & CAPITALISM

In his bestselling book, *Capital in the Twenty-First Century*, French economist Thomas Piketty raised the question, "Did even Jesus live in times of capitalism?" Although Piketty's examples and calculations go back to the year zero, his primary focus is data on wealth and income inequality in Europe and the US over the last 250 years.

Piketty believes that capitalism, though celebrated and admired, must be re-examined. Capitalism was not created, nor is it driven, by some external force. It is an economic model we created, one we've fed and supported, and to some extent it continues to work. But it is lacking compassion. For all his criticism, Piketty himself acknowledges being a capitalist, and as noted earlier, even the Dalai Lama believes in the model as long as we add a dash of compassion to the mix.

But, change is coming, and there are some major issues. The capitalist template as such is an OK thing, but it could be so much better with a healthy infusion of compassion. I personally would like to see an economic model that accommodates change, provides for on-going evolution and growth in the workplace, rewards the pursuit of wild knowledge, offers opportunity for all, and inspires confidence in a brighter tomorrow.

Change will come and it will have a profound impact on virtually all aspects of our lives. It will require a long-term focus on change-management and error-correction as we're swept along through the maelstrom of the 21st Century. We face enormous challenges. And yet, as always, with the challenges come tremendous opportunities. So, the simple question we need the answer to is, "Where are we heading?"

The corporate dinosaurs – the huge organizations, with their rigid hierarchies and monstrous bureaucracies – are dying. They're over-stuffed with people who are all very much alike. They have not embraced change, and are not equipped to do so. We will see technology start to chew off their inefficiencies. The machines will find the weak links, so you had better be prepared.

From a global perspective, half of the jobs we have today will be gone by 2060. And that will drive the emergence of many small, nimble, hyper-responsive businesses that master ever-more-specialized niches. We will become an increasingly interdependent, micro-capitalistic society, where countless small transactions occur. Large enterprises, with their all-encompassing approach, will have difficulty staying relevant and competing, and their demise will leave a gaping hole in the capitalist system we have today.

What will it mean to end the use of cash entirely and to restructure all of the rules, schemes, networks, systems and models that surround it? Computation will find efficient models and solutions for us. But cash plays an important role in our capitalist society – if not the physical cash, at least the value of money. "Cash is king," we have been taught. Capitalism is everything. Don't we all want to be wealthy? You have heard it so often: "The first million is the hardest one." There's no denying that having cash can make things easier. For entrepreneurs and companies, running short on financial resources is all too often a hard, cold reality. As the entrepreneur and venture capitalist Peter Thiel says in his terrific book, *Zero to One*, the purpose of any business is to generate positive cash flow. Entrepreneurs, in their search for credibility and investors, must have a plausible plan for making that happen, and larger organizations are always hustling for short-term returns to satisfy Wall Street.

When looking at the banking and financial services sectors, we can already see big changes taking shape. The costs associated with conducting cash transactions, filling automatic-teller machines, and keeping physical money safe and sound are much higher than the cost of managing virtual currency. And so, inevitably, cash will finally be done away with. The banks need to be bolder and actively force the change if they are to survive. The challenge is not to create the bank of the future, but rather to ask the question; do we even need banks in the future? Yes, employees will be let go. Sure, they will have to shut down physical office space and completely retool their modes of operation. The manual handling of routine transactions by people is one of the simplest things for technology to replace, so the banking industry will be hit faster and harder than one can imagine. We will maybe then finally learn to combine the two "isms" of our time, Humanism and Capitalism.

BYE BYE JOBS

The question of all questions, seems to be, "what will we be working with in future?" What about my Job? What will be the impact of 50% of all jobs disappearing (2 billion out of 4 billion jobs by 2060)? Historically, through the industrial revolution and other periods of wrenching change, we've been relatively good at replacing old jobs with new ones in new industries. But this was with "revolutions" and "paradigm shifts" that involved moving authorities from one group of human beings to another. Now, however, the authorities have moved into algorithms. Going forward into the future, jobs will be task-driven and every time you perform a task for someone, digital payment will be debited to your account. It will be a very different work/pay model.

The time-regulated jobs are dead, micro-invoicing and bookings are finished, and we should banish the thought of even having a job. The truth is we probably would not have adopted organizational hierarchies if we were more knowledgeable when we structured our economy some 250 years ago. We probably would not have the employer/employee relationships that we have today and everything would be task-driven – precisely what we're on the verge of seeing happen. Deconstruction of the old model will not be straightforward, it will not be easy, and glass will be broken. But this is where we need to start if we are to change our economic system to align with the realities of the future.

Still, I do not think we are ready for the kind of utopia that American author Daniel Pinchbeck describes in his book, *Breaking Open the Head*. He envisions a world where we move from pervasive oversight by paternalistic authorities to mass social sharing and volunteerism, all of which would free up peoples' real potential. And although, in the younger generation, I see a desire to work within open, participatory cultures, it is not obvious that they'll lead us to Pinchbeck's utopia.

That said, I have a really hard time thinking about a current job that can not theoretically be replaced by an algorithm. The simple logic behind this is that everything we have created – structures and models – only exists in our minds. We have thought it up and created models around it. It is not real. There are no companies or countries as such, we have just agreed on these models and they continue to work as long as we all agree on them. The only thing we can relate to in terms of "reality", even though for all we know we might already be living in some kind of illusion or virtual world, is that which has the capability of suffering or loving. Everything else we have made up and, therefore, chances are, it can be replicated and rebuilt through algorithms. So what will be then? In regards to the jobs most likely to be replaced in the short term are those where the economical impact is high, this is where the investments will be and therefore also hit first.

Still, we should not be worried, at least in short and mid-term the automation and introduction to AI will be beneficial, it will free us up. But, the core topic is, we simply do not know – the future will be created and it is up to every single one of us to outthink the revolution and create the world we want to live in. By doing so, we will be better off.

A GLOBAL
MODEL

In a connected and interdependent world, we also need to move towards global structures and models. One start is the heavily discussed universal, unconditional social income. Finland is leading the way, and I believe we should all jump on. Soon they will see the first signs of people, who were heavily dependent on the unemployment structures and the insecurity of a "day-to-day" living, feeling less stressed and therefore being able to create and contribute to society. The initial effects, at least for western world countries, I believe will be very positive. With social income, at least for starters, Europe can take a lead in probing and re-shaping the model for the world. We have long left the nation states and, though we are seeing some after-pains of nationalism, I believe this is a short-term view as we move towards global(-ization) inter-dependency. Needless to say, this universal model will impact how we live and do business. There will be new questions and challenges, the wild knowledge will flourish. And the guidance will again be found in philosophy, as tomorrow's leaders become the moderators of change.

But we need to be aware of the challenges with these models.

While they might look good, they also (at least in current structures) come with a flip-side. The countries heavily hit by automation will first be the countries we have lifted out of poverty. As productions and fabrics are moved back to the U.S. and to Europe, we are unlikely to see "social base income taxes" going back to these countries as a compensation. Still, we have to follow this path and work it out. So, what will be the solution? Let's cling on to 'Wild Knowledge' and outthink the revolution and let our creative potential and our ideas lead the way.

We will only succeed if the optimist outruns the pessimist, as technology keeps moving onward and upward at an ever-accelerating rate. The optimist's advantage is that he or she remains curious and is NOT resistant to change. Our brain is lazy, yet hides the potential. Never has the distance between the generations (40 and 20) been bigger and, as I stated, we now find the biggest challenge is for 50+ white men with tailor-made suits and ties in leading positions today to remain curious. We might think globalization has peaked, or is slowing down, but there is no evidence of that. Speed is the all-round driver in the 21st Century. For the foreseeable future, at least, complexity will increase and digitization will continue to ramp up… endlessly faster and faster.

Whether we have an optimistic or pessimistic view of the future, and regardless of how dramatically things are changing, human beings will still be in business. We stand before three radical changes, call them revolutions if you like, and right in front of us are new opportunities and challenges. It will never be how it was, the field of energy, the whole ecosystem around cities and our way of handling/working with consumption/circular economy will change our lives like we have never seen before. As entrepreneurs, executives, managers, and rank and file employees, we have the opportunity to spend the next dozen years taking control of and exploiting technology in order to master the 21st Century and become "Leaders of Change".

END NOTE

So, this was my calling — to be a businessman, an ex-hardcore capitalist, a thinker in the modern world, an explorer straddling the fields of science and technology, a team-builder, an agent of change, a proponent of strong, meaningful brands. I am fascinated by that place where Darwinian 'survival of the fittest' meets the sex appeal of brilliant branding. I am in my element when I'm engaged in the art of thinking, practising the art of philosophy, living the art of life, revelling in the pandemonium of wild knowledge.

I'll say it again: we need philosophy, now more than ever. Unlikely as it may seem, these are exciting times to be a philosopher. As we look back, and turn to the future, the question is not whether the old thoughts are correct, but rather how they can be deployed and effectively utilized in the 21st Century. What would Hume, Nietzsche, Marcus Aurelius, Seneca or Epictetus think if they were living today? It is problematic, in these hectic times, that we do not think, that we don't pause and reflect, that we just don't seem to have the time. As Goethe mused, "I am writing this long letter because I cannot find time to write a short one." That pretty much sums up our dilemma. It seems that access to virtually unlimited information prevents us from seeing the obvious, even when the answers are hidden in plain sight.

For leaders, everywhere, it all boils down to pairing the philosophy of the past with the scientific knowledge and technology of tomorrow and doing it from the heart.

Anders
Røros, January 2017

www.outthinktherevolution.com